The Winner's Guide to
RIVERBOAT GAMBLING

TRAVEL AND GAMBLING GUIDE

D1516207

Dedicated to my mother, an intrepid traveler and to the loving memory of my father, an avocational historian, from your son, an unrepentant gambler.

The Winner's Guide to
RIVERBOAT
GAMBLING

TRAVEL AND GAMBLING GUIDE

Ed Wilhite

- Gambling Research Institute -
Cardoza Publishing

Cardoza Publishing, publisher of **Gambling Research Institute** (GRI) books, is the foremost gaming and gambling publisher in the world with a library of more than 50 up-to-date and easy-to-read books and strategies.

These authoritative works are written by the top experts in their fields and with more than 3,500,000 books in print, represent the best-selling and most popular gaming books anywhere.

First Edition

Library of Congress Catalog Card No: 92-72311
ISBN: 0-940685-33-7

**Write for your <u>free</u> catalogue of gambling books
advanced and computer strategies.**

CARDOZA PUBLISHING
P.O. Box 1500, Cooper Station, New York, NY 10276 • (718)743-5229

Table of Contents

Illustrations, Tables & Charts

I. INTRODUCTION

Today the hottest action in the Midwest is on the exciting, new riverboat casinos - grand passenger cruisers with all of the gaming excitement of the most famous casinos in the world.

The Winner's Guide to Riverboat Gambling brings this whole new world to you: the history of riverboats, a complete guide to each riverboat and the surrounding sights and attractions, and, best of all, an easy-to-read guide to the games available including strategies to let you walk away a winner!

You'll learn about the evolution of these majestic floating palaces and the parts played by Robert Fulton, young lawyer Abraham Lincoln, the railroads, and the Civil War in the steamboat's 100 year history.

The travel section of this book presents all of the information you'll need to take a cruise on any one of the riverboats: phone numbers, prices and schedules, directions, where to park and what to expect on board. For each locale, you'll also find information on a variety of local sights, attractions, and entertainment so you can plan a weekend trip to any of the cities that host the floating casinos.

The Casino Games section shows you how to play and win at each of the games offered on the riverboats: Blackjack, Craps, Slot Machines, Video Poker, Roulette, Baccarat and the Big 6 wheel. For each game, the rules are explained, the odds of each bet are analyzed, and the optimum strategy is presented to increase your chances of beating the house and being a winner.

For the novice, to help put you at ease in this new setting, there are discussions of casino etiquette and the roles of casino employees.

The experienced gambler will find the latest, most complete strategies available for the rules offered on any of the riverboat casinos. But there is more than just the riverboat version of the games. You'll also learn about the rules and options that are available in Las Vegas and Atlantic City and the strategies that maximize your odds in every major casino in the United States!

And because winning requires more than just knowing the rules and odds of the game, we offer valuable money management tips that will help you keep your game under control and increase your chances of leaving your cruise with some of the casino's money.

The information in this book should be helpful to you in planning a cruise on one or more of the riverboats, but please be aware that any of these details, especially timing and prices, is subject to change, so don't make firm plans without verifying these particulars.

I would like to thank you for your interest in *The Winner's Guide to Riverboat Gambling*. A project of this type is rarely the product of one person, and I must recognize Keith Blomberg for the maps contained herein and Diane Garrison and Bruce Nims for their research and reporting help. Avery Cardoza of Cardoza Publishing provided invaluable assistance making the gaming portions of the book both more concise and more comprehensive. Thank you, all. Any errors or omissions that remain are strictly my responsibility.

The riverboat casinos carry over 100,000 passengers each week. The average gambler has only a vague grasp of the odds he faces and loses almost $60 on a cruise. That's the average gambler.

But after you read this book, you'll be a smart gambler, and with proper play, a winner. I hope you enjoy both *The Winner's Guide* and your cruise on one of the new riverboat casinos!

- *Ed Wilhite*

II. THE STORY OF THE RIVERBOATS

The History of the Riverboats in America

One of the most enduring images in American history has to be that of the Mississippi River steamboat. In a flash you can conjure up the image of slaves carrying cotton bales onto the loading ramp of the steamboat sitting alongside the dock.

Or perhaps you see a woodcut of the famous race between the Robert E. Lee and the Natchez. Or maybe the picture in your mind's eye is the Cotton Belle, the Show Boat of musical and movie fame. Or do you see Huck Finn and Jim poling their raft downstream desperately trying to get out of the way of a steamboat on its way from New Orleans carrying a load of freight and passengers to St. Louis?

For almost 100 years the steamboat was the king of the river, plying its trade along the Mississippi River system, which includes the Arkansas, Ohio, Missouri, and Illinois Rivers along with The Big Muddy. Not only were the huge boats a practical, cheap way to get goods up and down the rivers, they were majestic. They had presence and character and fired one's imagination.

Samuel Clemens, later to become famous as Mark Twain, grew up in Hannibal, Missouri, along the Mississippi in the 1830's and 40's. As a young man, he paid $500 for a position as an apprentice steamboat pilot and earned his pilot's license.

Some years later, he used his experiences in *Life on the Mississippi*, a fascinating rendering of the era of the steamboat. Here is Twain's description of the steamboat:

"And the boat is rather a handsome sight, too. She is long and sharp and trim and pretty; she has two tall, fancy-topped chimneys, with a gilded device of some kind swung between them; a fanciful pilot-house, all glass and 'gingerbread,' perched on top of the 'texas' deck behind them; the paddleboxes are gorgeous with a picture or with gilded rays above the boat's name; the boiler deck, the hurricane deck, and the texas deck are fenced and ornamented with clean white

9

railings; there is a flag gallantly flying from the jack-staff; the furnace doors are open and the fires glaring bravely; the upper decks are black with passengers, the captain stands by the big bell, calm, imposing, the envy of all; great volumes of the blackest smoke are rolling and tumbling out of the chimneys - a husbanded grandeur created with a bit of pitch pine just before arriving at a town; the crew are grouped on the forecastle; the broad stage is run far out over the port bow, and an envied deck-hand stands picturesquely on the end of it with a coil of rope in his hand; the pent steam is screaming through the gauge-cocks; the captain lifts his hand, a bell rings, the wheels stop; then they turn back, churning the water to foam, and the steamer is at rest. . . ."

The Earliest Steamboats

We all learned in school that Robert Fulton invented the steamship in 1807 when he launched his first successful, steam-powered vessel, officially *The North River Steamboat*, better known as the *Clermont* and as *Fulton's Folly*.

What Fulton had done was make minor improvements on the efforts of other inventors of his time and modify a deep-keeled ocean-going ship by removing the masts, putting boilers and engines below the deck, and mounting 2 large paddle wheels, one on each side of the ship, for motive power. The design was excellent for the deeper waters of Hudson Bay, the Erie Canal, and the Great Lakes.

Fulton teamed up with Robert Livingston and they proceeded to acquire exclusive landing rights at "public" docks first along the Eastern waterways, then the Ohio, and finally along the Mississippi from Rock Island, Illinois to New Orleans. By 1814, their monopoly on carrying freight up-river was complete.

Downriver was no big deal. Anyone could build a raft or flatboat, hire a friend or two as a crew, and float downstream with a couple of tons of grain or manufactured goods bound for Memphis, Natchez, or New Orleans.

The trick was getting bales of cotton back upstream. Fulton-Livingston had control of that end of the business, and since they could charge high rates to carry cotton upstream, they could charge low rates to carry goods south if it was required to undercut possible competition.

The drawback they faced was the design of Fulton's boats. Because of their deep keel, they needed at least 15 feet of water to travel safely.

The Mississippi of the time was an untamed river - there were literally dozens of bends per mile south of Cairo, Illinois; there were places where the channel might be almost completely jammed with logs and debris for hundreds of yards; and there were reaches, straight stretches of river where the water ran deep and fast.

In order to be assured of the clearance needed, Fulton's ships had to travel in the center of the river where the current was the strongest. A trip from New Orleans to St. Louis took as long as 30 days.

If the Fulton-style steamships had remained the only steam-powered packets on the rivers, they would have played a brief, insignificant role in the history of the midwestern rivers.

As soon as the railroads expanded into the region the reign of the steamship would have ended.

It wouldn't even take that long.

From out of Pittsburgh, came Henry Miller Shreve, the Father of the Steamboat. He designed and built a broad-bottomed vessel that had a shallow draft. By putting his furnaces, boilers, and engines up on the deck, he was able to design his steamboat to draw as little as five feet of water.

Boats built along the lines of Shreve's steamboat could stay nearer the banks of the river where the current was weaker. They could take short-cuts behind islands and through cut-offs that their deeper-drawing sister ships could not take advantage of. In short, Shreve's boats travelled on the water instead of in it.

In the Spring of 1819, Captain Shreve, then 35 years old, steamed into New Orleans and effectively broke the Fulton-Livingston monopoly within a matter of days. His first steamboat, the Enterprise, made the run from New Orleans to St. Louis in fifteen days.

The shippers in New Orleans, swayed by the savings from the faster boats, pressured their legislature to end the Fulton-Livingston's hold on steam/freight shipping. The steamboat was the wave of the future on the rivers. The steamship was relegated to the coasts and the Great Lakes.

Captain Shreve dedicated his life to the riverboats and river travel. He invented a double-hulled boat with a large derrick in front to allow its crew to pull logs out of the water and saw them into harmless lengths. His "snag-killers" worked up and down the rivers during the 1820's until log jams were almost a thing of the past, except during the Spring floods when new-fallen trees were swept away in the high water. In 1839 he founded a town on the Red River at the spot where an army depot was being disbanded.

Today Shreveport, Louisiana is the third largest city in the state.

Boom Times for Steamboats

When the fates are kind enough to provide an ideal solution to a pressing problem, there is liable to be explosive growth in the area and lots of money changing hands.

The steamboats were a perfect example of this phenomenon. Within two years of Shreve's maiden voyage into New Orleans, sixty steamboats were built. Over the next fifty years, over 6000 steamboats would be constructed, 2000 intended for the Mississippi alone, the rest for her major tributaries.

The average steamboat cost about $50,000 at that time to build and outfit. Yet the profits from hauling freight were so great that an owner could expect to pay for his boat within one year. And, make no mistake about it, freight was the reason to build the big boats. As we shall see, the steamers carried passengers, but for the most part, it was freight that provided the volume and the money to support the growing steamboat business.

It was essential that the boats be able to pay for themselves quickly because the average life of a riverboat was three years. Most were wrecked on sandbars or snags, a large number suffered fires or boiler explosions, and not a few sank after collisions with another boat.

"Get in, get your payback, and hope for a few more months" was the motto of the packet owners up and down the rivers.

The hazards of the river cannot be over-estimated. There were no locks or dams to control and level out the flow of water; there were no lights or buoys along the midwestern rivers until 1875; there was no Army Crops of Engineers to dredge and maintain a channel. Change was the only thing constant about the rivers during the 19th century, and the success of the riverboat trade was due almost solely to the skill of the men (there were no licensed women pilots) who became steamboat pilots.

An apprentice pilot or "cub" generally spent two years acquiring the necessary skills of his trade. Learning to steer the boat took about an hour; the rest of the training was designed to teach the new pilot to know his river, or at least a portion of it, for pilots were only licensed for specified lengths on specific rivers.

The pilot had to know the river better than he knew the back of his hand. Both upstream and down, in daylight, dark, dawn, and dusk, he had to know the location of every bend, island, point, sandbar, and snag along the entire length of the voyage. Or, at least, he had to know where those things had been a few days ago, because the river was rarely the same from one trip to the next.

Mark Twain wrote,

"Two things seemed pretty apparent to me. One was, that in order to be a pilot a man had got to learn more than any one man ought to be allowed to know; and the other was, that he must learn it all over again in a different way every twenty-four hours."

Supplementing his eyes and memory, the pilot gained his most useful information from soundings taken off the river's bottom at his request. When he wanted readings taken, the pilot would ring the bell as a signal to the "leadsman" who hurried to the prow of the boat with a rope with a lead weight on the end and knots (or other markers woven into the rope) every six feet.

The leadsman would lower the weighted end into the water and sing out the depth in terms of 'marks' along the rope. *Mark four* meant twenty-four feet of water, absolute safety in the riverboat world. *Mark twain (two)* was twelve feet, plenty of water, but don't get overconfident. *Quarter less twain* meant one-fourth of a mark less than twelve feet (9 1/2 feet), definitely something to watch. And *mark one* indicated six feet of water and trouble was imminent.

The steamboat had the power to back itself off of a sand or mud bar if it got grounded, but the real risk was that it would run into a stump or submerged log and tear open its hull.

Each steamboat had a captain, often the owner, who was the master of the boat, crew, and cargo while they were docked. Once they began a journey, the pilot was absolute ruler of the entire vessel. Of course he was still the employee of the owner, and his tenure might be short if he and the owner/captain did not see eye to eye on many matters.

There were two other skilled positions on the crew of the steamer - relief pilot and engineer. The pilots stood four-hour watches alternately for the duration of the trip so there were two licensed pilots on each boat.

The engineer was responsible for the mechanical equipment of the boat. His was the task of maintaining the boilers and engines at all times. The engineer was responsible for about one-half of the crew of two dozen or so roustabouts. His crew of firemen were charged with keeping up a full head of steam, lubricating fittings and bearings, and keeping the boilers filled with clean water.

The deck hands were primarily busy when the packet made a stop. They had to load and store cargo and supplies and keep the boat supplied with lengths of wood for the boiler. Most often a steamer would stock up with cords of freshly cut wood when it made its regularly scheduled stops.

But as the business became more competitive and scheduling was tightened, the pilots were reluctant to stop for wood, so they merely lashed on a barge filled with fresh fuel and headed on upstream. The roustabouts transferred the wood to the deck on the fly, then cut the empty barge loose and let it float back to its owner.

It should be noted that the roustabouts were generally hired employees except that a steamer which confined its routes to the Southern rivers might have some slaves in her crew, at least before the

14

Civil War.

Freight paid for the steamboats. They hauled bales of cotton from the river cities of the South to the industrial areas of the midwest. On the return trips downstream, the boats would carry manufactured goods, grain (and its principal by-product, alcohol), hides and furs. But if freight were the only reason for the big boats, they would quickly have evolved to be more like barges than like the floating palaces that they became.

For the steamboats also carried passengers: plantation owners with their families, businessmen, ranchers from Texas and Arkansas, con men of all sorts, prostitutes, and, of course, gamblers.

Most boats had both first class accommodations with something resembling a private stateroom and deck class, where the passenger provided his own blanket and food and scrounged for a place to sleep. A typical first class journey from St Louis to New Orleans was $50 while deck class might cost $8.

The passengers were responsible for their own amusement, and if a boat was loaded with freight, they might find that choices were severely limited. Card games (generally mis-named "games of chance") were common. Prostitution was generally frowned upon, but, as in many climates, a blind eye was turned to a discrete woman plying the trade. At worst she could expect to be dropped off at the next stop.

The Long Decline

Just as the steamboats forced the steamships off the rivers of middle America, so too did the railroads provide serious competition for the steamers. For a while the railroads tended to run East and West between major cities while the principle river traffic was North-South.

But a train could travel the distance between New Orleans and Memphis in less than a day, and it took the boats three days at best. It was a just a matter of time.

The first railroad reached the Mississippi River in 1854 at Rock Island, Illinois, and in 1856 they built the first bridge across the river to continue on to Kansas City. Within days, an old steamboat, the Effie Afton, crashed into the bridge and burned. The Effie's owners sued the railroad for obstructing navigation. The railroad hired an Illinois attorney to defend their choice of location and type of bridge, and Abe Lincoln was able to persuade the court that the bridge was not an obstruction.

In April, 1861, the Civil War broke out and two things happened which spelled the doom of the freight-carrying steamboats. First, the rivers were divided North and South. There was no longer traffic along the 900 miles of the Mississippi. It was restricted to either portion of the river starting at Cairo, Illinois.

Hundreds of boats were burned as the Northern troops moved to re-take the Mississippi River.

And secondly, while steamboat traffic was held back, railway use had explosive growth. Rail beds were laid, trestles were built, freight cars and freight handling procedures were improved as both sides used the railroads to help them fight the war.

After Appomattox, the Southern economy was in a shambles. For several years they had virtually no goods to trade nor money with which to purchase items from the North. As trade slowly recovered, it was the railroads that carried it. As a result, the surviving steamboats concentrated on passenger traffic.

Of course, the trains could (and did) carry people, and the train trip was faster. But there are always some for whom speed is not the issue; comfort and style are. And the steamboats developed a definite style.

As less space was required for freight, more and more room on the steamboats was given over to the staterooms and lounges that gave the impression of comfortable travel. The common areas evolved with a sort of "steamboat baroque": lots of ornate, carved woodwork, gilding, stained glass, and generally over-done glitz and glitter. The steam calliope was introduced in 1858, and by the end of the war, every steamer had at least one.

Behind these public areas, it was most often the case that a rustic simplicity still ruled. Cabins were likely to be stark with bunk beds, a wash basin, and little else.

On board there were two areas where boats would visibly compete with one another: meals and entertainment. The dining situation reached the point of absurdity in the 1870's. Each meal would consist of up to thirty to forty courses with six kinds of meat, five varieties of fish, soups, vegetables, salads, fruits, nuts, breads, and a variety of desserts.

Entertainment made the transition from 'unauthorized' to official. An owner would hire an acting group, a singer, or a lecturer/comedian to fill some of the idle hours on the trip, which still took three to four times longer than the comparable train ride.

The keenest competition between boats, the competition that raised the most interest among not only passengers but the public at large, was racing. Boats would race against the clock to set the speed record for travel between two cities. Occasionally two boats would actually race each other, matching pilot against pilot for navigational skills and crew against crew to shave seconds off of the time required to make a stop, off-load and load parcels and passengers, pick up a fuel barge, and take off again.

A captain who would not at least attempt to make record-breaking runs was likely to find that the business was going to other vessels whose owners were a bit more sporting.

The most famous race took place in June, 1870, between the Natchez and the Robert E Lee. The Natchez had just broken the ultimate speed record, for the trip from New Orleans to St Louis. Upon her return to New Orleans, the captain of the Robert E Lee issued an informal challenge, saying that he intended to beat the Natchez and break the record on this trip.

The race took several days and all along the Mississippi River, spectators would flock to the banks to see the boats pass. All in all, it had to be one of the dullest sporting events to gain such attention: both boats averaged about fourteen miles an hour (peaking at twenty mph), the Robert E Lee took the lead at the start and never relinquished it, and except for the first few miles near New Orleans, both boats were never visible at the same time.

But it was a race, and the Robert E Lee set the record for paddlewheelers that was never broken - 3 days, 18 hours, and 14 minutes.

In spite of these moments of glory, the decline was inevitable and inexorable. The four-blade propeller was patented in 1836, and propeller-driven barges were both faster and cheaper than the steamboats. They began to usurp what freight traffic there was left on the rivers. George Pullman invented his famous sleeping cars in 1863 and dining cars in 1868 which helped make the railroads a more civilized way to travel. The steamers had to find new, and smaller, niches to stay financially afloat.

The end of the nineteenth century and the early years of the twentieth saw the rise and decline of the 'show boat'.

An old paddle-wheeler would make a tour, stopping at various town and cities presenting vaudeville, semi-serious theater, musical entertainment, and/or a circus. Often these boats used a propeller for propulsion and the paddle-wheels turned just for show. Or in the worst case, the big wheels were completely non-functional, and the boat was pushed along its route by a 'mule' ship.

By the 1930's there were only a handful of steamboats in the country, acting as excursion boats or as floating museums. The day of the steam-powered paddle-wheel had ended, and one of the most colorful bits of our history became history.

THE RIVERBOAT CASINOS TODAY

We have followed the evolution of the riverboat from freighter to luxury passenger liner to entertainment center to the excursion boat of today.

There are a few excursion boats still around: the Delta Queen and the Mississippi Queen, for instance, but they aren't steamboats. And several river cities have permanently docked, former steamboats that have been converted to restaurants, so a visitor can sample the experience of a riverboat.

But, all in all, the steam/riverboat would have to have been considered a page in American history that was finished. Finished, that is, until the Iowa state legislature, in April, 1989, passed a bill authorizing riverboat gambling along the Mississippi River border of

Iowa.

By licensing a limited number of floating casinos, Iowa hopes to stimulate tourism and jobs in its depressed riverfront areas, and, by taxing a portion of the riverboats' gambling income, they hope to provide another source of revenue for the state's education fund. The law took effect on April 1, 1991.

The Iowa law allows betting on certain carefully defined casino games with an upper limit of $5 per bet and a maximum loss per player of $200 on a (three or four hour) cruise. An individual must be 18 or older to enter the casino.

These limitations evolved for two reasons:

1. Iowa was the first state to experiment with this type of legislation, thus they did not have anyone to copy.

2. They hoped to minimize the Las Vegas image of free-wheeling gambling that higher limits might encourage. A seasoned gambler, much less a high-roller, is not going to be tempted by those betting limits unless it is the only game in town. Although, as any Iowa casino booster is likely to remind you, "There is no limit on how much you can win."

Illinois, which shares a long stretch of the Mississippi River with Iowa and has its own share of depressed river towns, quickly passed similar legislation. Early versions of the bill provided for a $500 cap on gambling losses (as opposed to Iowa's $200), but the final act omitted any limitations, either per bet or overall.

And, in the spirit of competition, Illinois' law allowed riverboat casinos to begin operation on January 1, 1991, a full four months before Iowa. Aside from some points scored in the press, however, Illinois' intentions were all for naught: the first Iowa riverboat casino opened on April 1, 1991, while the first Illinois boat was launched on September 10, 1991.

The Illinois legislation provides for up to 20 casinos on the rivers in and bordering the state. As of mid-1992, there are four Illinois riverboat casinos in operation with four additional Illinois boats scheduled to hit the water by the end of 1993. Iowa has three riverboats in operation and Mississippi has two.

19

The other states along the Mississippi River were not sleeping through this two-year period between the debate over the first riverboat gambling bill and the launch of the first riverboat casino. In 1991, Louisiana and Mississippi legalized versions of riverboat gambling within their boundaries, with new boats expected to be launched in 1993. Unlike the other states, Mississippi actually allows permanently docked "boats", a casino that just happens to have a wet basement. Both Louisiana and Mississippi followed Illinois' lead in allowing no limit gambling.

Missouri will have a public referendum on riverboat gambling in November, 1992, and Arkansas and Kansas are considering legislation to get into the act.

For the states, there are two huge appeals to riverboat gambling: it is a source of jobs and a source of revenue.

Each riverboat is a tourist attraction with a staff of telephone-reservation clerks, ticket takers, restaurant and bar workers; a casino requiring a large staff of dealers, pit bosses, security personnel and cashiers; and a company with a back office operation including marketing, accounting, personnel and other staff.

These jobs didn't exist before the riverboat went into operation. In the towns where the boats dock, restaurants, service stations, and souvenir shops either open or expand to handle the increased volume of tourists drawn to the boats. All of these newly employed or busier people spend money in the area, creating still more jobs and opportunities.

Clearly there is a limit to how many riverboat casinos an area can support, but while a single boat may employ 500 people, the rippling effects can account for up to 2000 additional jobs in the region - from just one riverboat.

The states enjoy other benefits beyond the increased employment generated by the presence of the casinos. All of these employees pay taxes in their state. Boarding fees charged by the boats include a dollar or two for the state. The tourist dollars generate sales tax revenue. Tourists buy gas and increase the fuel tax receipts. And the states have carefully designed a variety of ways to extract money from the gambling itself.

For instance, there is a fee just to apply for a license. In Illinois, an applicant (with no guarantee of securing a license) pays a $50,000 non-refundable fee to have that application reviewed. Finally, the largest portion of the revenue that the states collect comes from a percentage of the gross revenue of the casinos.

Each state has its own formula, but the bottom line is that from 5% to 20% of the casinos' gross revenue is turned over to the local Department of Revenue. As with the lotteries in many states, most of the revenue from riverboat gambling is targeted for education.

After the first several months, the boats averaged about 70% of capacity with revenues to the states being almost twice what was initially projected. The average passenger loses about $60 on a 3-hour cruise.

Thousands of jobs have been created, but, because most of the gamblers live within 60 miles of the boat they frequent, this gain in new jobs is partially offset by some lost jobs in other recreational businesses.

As the riverboat gambling industry matures and there are more boats in tourist destination cities such as St Louis and New Orleans, the region should see real gains as dollars are attracted from outside the area.

The cities themselves have found that the boats are not an unalloyed positive contribution. The increase in tax revenues is tempered by the disruption of construction, pressure on available parking, and increased property taxes on business near the river. Merchants complain that gamblers drive to town, take a cruise, and leave; they have not seen the increased business for which they had hoped.

But for whatever motives and through whatever process, the riverboat gambling industry has been created. Boats were converted from other uses or built from scratch to meet the demand that various entrepreneurs anticipate. For better or worse, riverboat gambling is here to stay.

III. RIVERBOAT & TRAVELLING GUIDE

The following information should be helpful to you in planning a cruise on one or more of the riverboats, but please be aware that any of these details, especially timing and prices, is subject to change. Don't make firm plans without verifying the information presented here.

Also be aware that your riverboat may not actually leave the dock during your cruise. During the winter season, roughly from November through March, and often in inclement weather, you may spend the entire trip dockside or standing by. This does not affect the gambling on board, but it does make for a monotonous view if you had hoped to see the scenery.

ILLINOIS' RIVERBOAT CASINOS

> ### ALTON BELLE CASINO
> **Alton, Illinois**
> 1-800-336-7568 (1-800-336-SLOT)

Games: 300 Slot Machines, Blackjack, Craps, Big 6
Schedule: Cruises every 3 hours starting at 9:00 am.
Price: From $8 to $20, depending upon time, day, and season
Opened: September, 1991

Location and Directions
Alton is on the Illinois side of the Mississippi River just north of

St Louis. In Illinois take Routes 100 or 67 to get to Alton and take Rt 67 to the river. From St Louis, take Rt 67 across the Lewis and Clark Bridge and follow the signs.

The Alton Belle docks at the Alton Landing, located where Rt 67 turns left along the river. There is plenty of free parking within 100 yards of the Alton Landing.

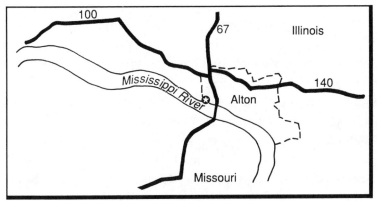

The Boat and Your Cruise

The Alton Belle is the most 'single purpose' of the casino boats; she is a casino. Period. No restaurants (though sandwiches are available), no entertainment, no family activities. There are two bars, 3 decks of casino games, and a few chairs in which to lounge and enjoy the view. You must be at least 21 to board.

The Main Deck is entirely devoted to Slot Machines. If you can locate the narrow stairway or the elevator, you will find the table games on the two upper decks.

The top level is especially nice - a sort of sun room with a few Blackjack tables. It is by far the best place to play and watch the beautiful limestone bluffs drift past.

Be warned, however, that if your cruise is crowded, the minimum limits will be higher on these tables. Generally the minimum bet at Blackjack is $5 at most of the tables on board. The minimum bet for Craps is usually $10, but it can be as high as $25 at peak cruise times.

Reservations are recommended for the most popular cruises: weekday mid-days and weekend afternoon and nights. A cruise actually lasts about two and one-half hours, and you are allowed to board 30 minutes prior to departure.

Gambling is available when you board, not when the Alton Belle departs, and you should make it a point to pull yourself away from the action for a few minutes to watch the landscape drift by. This stretch of the Mississippi River has miles of impressive limestone bluffs.

Local Sights and Entertainment

If you are an antique buff, it is easy to spend the rest of the day wandering around the streets within a few blocks of Alton Landing. There are over 50 antique stores in town, offering a truly awesome variety of furniture, clocks, and collectibles. Some of the stores double as a small restaurant, putting their antique tables and chairs to good use until sold.

Just across the Mississippi, the whole of St Louis awaits you. The Gateway Arch, the world famous St Louis Zoo, the Art Institute, Anheuser-Busch Brewery, Busch Stadium, Six Flags, the Bowling Hall of Fame (some people go there), the Science Center, and dozens of other museums and attractions are within minutes of the Alton Belle.

PAR-A-DICE RIVERBOAT CASINO
Peoria, Illinois
1-800-332-5634 for information;
Ticket Master for reservations.

Games: 500 Slot Machines, Blackjack, Craps, Roulette, Big 6, Mini-Baccarat
Schedule: Every three hours starting at 8:30 am
Price: From $5 to $10
Opened: November, 1991

Location and Directions
If you want to get to Par-a-Dice (they just LOVE it when people

say that), get on I-74 and take Exit 93 onto Washington St. Turn left onto Main Street and follow the signs. Parking at the Spirit of Peoria Landing is $4, or parking is available on the streets within a block or two.

In the Fall of 1992, Par-a-Dice is scheduled to relocate to permanent docking facilities on the east side of the Illinois River about one-half mile upstream of its current site.

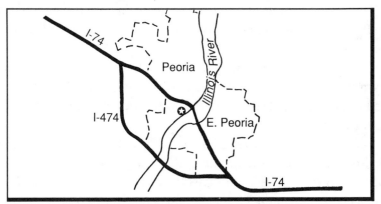

The Boat and Your Cruise

Par-a-Dice has four decks (three open to passengers). On the Main Deck is a casino devoted entirely to Slot Machines and a bar. The Boiler Deck has some Slot Machines and 28 gaming tables, and the Texas Deck is a third casino area with table games, more Slot Machines and a snack Bar.

The term *Texas Deck* is a holdover from historic riverboat days. The captain's stateroom was named Texas because it was more spacious than the other rooms. Eventually the term was applied to the whole deck where the captain's quarters could be found.

During the summer months, there is a bar on the open-air Hurricane Deck. Each enclosed deck has restrooms and some outside space if you want to get away from the smoke. The boat has a listed capacity of 1200, but if it is that full, you will find that it is quite crowded. You will have a more pleasant experience if you go on the off times.

The Slot Machines are quarter, $1, and $5. At the tables, the minimum bet tends to be $5, but you can also find $10, $25 and $50 Blackjack games if the crowd is large. Drinks are $1 each for gamblers.

Local Sights and Entertainment

Peoria is the third largest city in Illinois with an area population of 225,000. It is roughly 150 miles southwest of Chicago and 160 miles north of St Louis. The city boasts a full range of restaurants and night spots plus the athletic and entertainment offerings of Bradley University.

If you wish to continue your gambling in an entirely different environment, there is a deluxe Off Track Betting (OTB) Parlor where you can place legal bets on several horse races occurring across the country.

If you want to get away from the hustle of the city, visit Wildlife Prairie Park with its zoo, frontier village, and craft shops ten miles west of downtown Peoria. In East Peoria is the historic site of Fort Crevecoeur, the original French settlement in the Peoria area.

During late September, check out Rendezvous Days in the Fort Crevecoeur Park.

```
CASINO ROCK ISLAND
Rock Island, Illinois
1-800-477-7747 for reservations
(1-800-477-8946 for groups)
```

Games: 400 Slot Machines, Blackjack, Craps, Roulette, Big 6
Schedule: Cruises depart every 3 hours starting at 7:00am.
Prices: $9 to $14
Opened: March, 1992

Location and Directions

220 miles north of St Louis, straddling the Mississippi River, one finds the Quad Cities: Bettendorf and Davenport, Iowa, and Moline

and Rock Island, Illinois. The Quad Cities are home to two riverboat casinos including the Casino Rock Island and one boat located on the Iowa side of the River. This boat will be featured in the Iowa section.

Interstates 74 and 80 lead to the Quad Cities. To find the Casino Rock Island, take Rt 67 or 92 to their intersection at the Centennial Bridge. The Casino Rock Island staging area is at The Boatworks, a couple of hundred yards south on Rt 92.

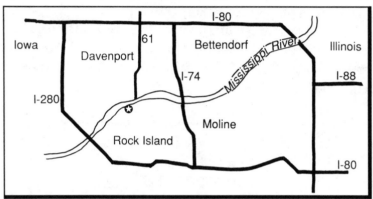

The Boat and Your Cruise

The first thing you will notice is that there are four boats here, three permanently docked. The Casino Rock Island is a sternwheel paddleboat built as a casino. The Ockerson is a river museum and the Effie Afton (named after the riverboat that crashed into the first bridge over the Mississippi 135 years ago) is a 300-person restaurant.

Boarding time for each cruise is 15 minutes before departure time, and you will return to dock about thirty minutes before the next departure. There are no restaurant facilities on board the Casino Rock Island, but your fare does include a deli buffet available on each cruise.

Local Sights and Entertainment

In the Quad Cities area, it is very easy to experience the difference in gambling philosophy of these two states; you will be able to bet as little as twenty-five cents at the Slot Machines or as much as $1000 per hand/roll/throw at the tables.

Spend the afternoon seeing some of the sights in the area, then take an evening cruise in Iowa on the President (Davenport) and enjoy a great dinner there.

You'll find that the $5 maximum bet allowed in Iowa makes for a very different atmosphere without the stress of high-stakes gaming.

Between boat rides you may want to check out the Ockerson River Museum (Rock Island), the Children's Museum (Bettendorf), or the Putnam Museum of History (Davenport).

For the sports (or sporting) minded, there is horse racing at Quad City Downs (East Moline) from April to October. Also recommended are the Niabi Zoological Park and the Bix Beiderbeck Memorial Jazz Festival in July.

SILVER EAGLE
East Dubuque, Illinois
1-800-723-2453

Games: Blackjack, Craps, Roulette, 470 Slot Machines
Schedule: 2 1/2 hour cruises departing every 3 hours from 8:30am until 11:30pm
Prices: $6 to $12
Opened: June, 1992

Location and Directions

East Dubuque is at the far northwestern corner of Illinois where Illinois meets Iowa and Wisconsin. The Silver Eagle docks at the Frentress Lake Marina, on Route 20 ten miles north of Galena and about five minutes south of the bridge that takes you into Dubuque, Iowa. You literally can't miss it from Highway 20.

At dockside is the Eagle's Nest Pavilion which houses the ticket office, a restaurant, sandwich shop, and souvenir shop.

The Silver Eagle folks are also providing introductory classes on the rules and etiquette of their casino games, and they are offering child care on site because Illinois law states that you must be 21 to board a riverboat casino. As an added touch, there is valet parking for all guests of the casino.

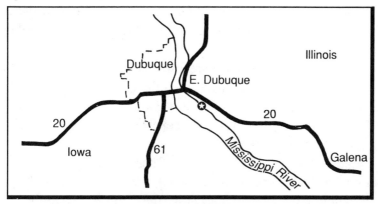

The Boat and Your Cruise

The Silver Eagle was newly constructed as a riverboat casino, and she is not designed along the lines of the historic Mississippi riverboat. There are no smokestacks or paddlewheels on the Silver Eagle. She has the more rounded lines of an excursion boat that you might find on Lake Michigan.

You may enjoy gambling action on any of three enclosed decks or work your way to the open platform on top to take in some scenery.

There is no restaurant on the Silver Eagle but you will find bar service on each deck and a small lounge area where you can order sandwiches and hot hors d'oeuvres. The lounge area has plenty of windows to provide maximum view.

The Main Deck is all Slot Machines and Video Poker games. On the upper two gaming decks, you will find more Slots plus the table games: Blackjack, Craps, and Roulette. Minimum bets at most of the tables are $5, but you can find the occasional $3 table at off-peak times. The maximum bet is $1000.

Local Sights and Entertainment

East Dubuque and Galena are in a region rich in history. Almost 200 years ago, lead and zinc were discovered in the area, and the wealth from these natural resources was transformed into beautiful homes, churches and public buildings, many of which are preserved today.

Galena was also the home of Ulysses S Grant, Commander-in-Chief of the Union Army during the Civil War and President of the United States.

Throughout the year, there are festivals and fairs centered on the various historic aspects northwestern Illinois. Of particular note are the Summer and Fall Tours of Historic Homes in Galena (mid-June and late September). During these weekends, you can also take a free lamplight tour of U S Grant's home.

Eight miles south of Galena is the Chestnut Mountain Ski Area. During the Winter, Chestnut offers a full service ski facility including night skiing and snowmobiling. During the Summer, it is worth a visit to Chestnut for a ride on the Alpine Slide, a wheeled sled on a bobsled-like track.

Mostly you will want to amble among the dozens of shops and galleries in the towns of this area. Many artists and artisans have gravitated here, and you can find anything from hand-made soap to a hand-carved piano.

THE EMPRESS
Joliet, Illinois
708-345-6789

Games: 607 Slot Machines, Blackjack, Craps, Roulette, Big 6
Schedule: unknown at this time
Prices: $8 to $15
Opened: scheduled to launch July, 1992

Location and Directions

The Empress is a boat on a river, but she is not a riverboat in the traditional meaning of the word. You won't find Mark Twain imitators or smokestacks or fresh-from-the-plantation Southern accents here.

The Empress is a sleek, modern catamaran on the Des Plains River in Joliet, about 40 miles from the Chicago Loop. From I-80 just east of I-55, take the Larkin Exit south and follow the signs. Parking is $4.

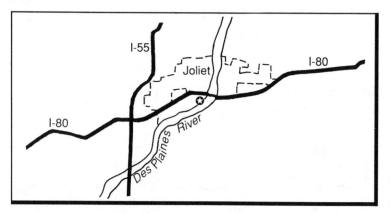

The Boat and Your Cruise

The Empress has 2 enclosed decks that are all casino action and an open air deck on top if you want to get away from the games. There is bar service and some snacks available but no real dining or alternative entertainment facilities on board.

You will find a restaurant and large shopping area on shore adjacent to the Empress' mooring spot. It is anticipated that cruises will last approximately 3 hours.

Local Sights and Entertainment

Joliet is a city of 80,000 that is just far enough from Chicago not to be considered a suburb. If you are going to spend some time in and around Joliet, try to take in some of the outdoor opportunities that the area offers.

Starved Rock State Park is about forty miles west, near Ottawa. Also worth a visit is the Illinois and Michigan Canal Museum Complex in Lockport, about ten miles north.

If you can't get enough action on board the Empress, you will find horse racing from April until October at Balmoral Race Track (at the intersection of Rts 1 and 394, thirty-five miles East).

Joliet also offers an abundance of parks, conservation areas, bicycle trails, and campgrounds.

CITY LIGHTS I AND CITY LIGHTS II
Aurora, Illinois
1-708-801-0330

Games: Slot Machines, Blackjack, Craps, Roulette, Baccarat
Schedule: nothing known yet
Prices: nothing known yet
Opened: scheduled for June, 1993

One of the Atlantic City casinos is planning to open two riverboat casinos in the Summer of 1993 on the Fox River in Aurora, Illinois. The boats will feature gaming (and bar service) only, with restaurant facilities on shore.

Each boat will have two enclosed decks for the casino areas and an open air deck topside. The boats are going to be small by existing riverboat casino standards: capacity will be 500 and 545 passengers.

Aurora is a southwestern suburb of Chicago - about thirty-five miles from the Loop. From Route 5, exit at Rt 31 and head south to the riverfront in downtown Aurora. Both boats will be docked there.

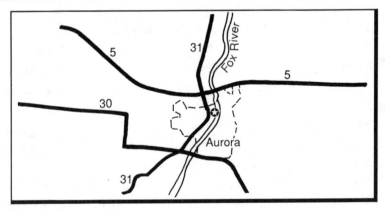

Local Sights and Entertainment

If you are planning to spend a day or two in the Aurora area, you may want to check out the Aurora Transportation Center with its reconstructed, pre-Civil War, stone, railroad roundhouse.

In March check out the Sugar Maple Fest, and, if you are in Aurora in June, Band Organ Day is not to be missed.

Just ten miles northwest is the Fermi National Accelerator, and an hour's drive or less will get you to almost anywhere in the Chicago metroplex, where you can see and do almost everything possible at some time or other.

OTHER ILLINOIS RIVERBOATS

The Illinois law provides for up to twenty riverboats to be licensed in the state. To date, no more than ten of these licenses have been approved. One license has been reserved for East St Louis, but at this writing no group has been able to combine the financing and the credentials needed to obtain approval for the East St Louis license.

Other sites under consideration include: Metropolis (near Paducah, Kentucky) on the Ohio River and a second riverboat in Joliet on the Des Plaines River. For information about the progress of any of these or other potential boats, call the Illinois Department of Travel and Tourism (see Appendix 1).

It seems likely that if the state's share of the revenue from riverboat gambling continues to exceed projections, that the definition of 'river' is likely to be expanded to include Lake Michigan (Chicago) and some of the downstate recreational lakes (Springfield, Shelbyville, Carlyle, Rend, or Crab Orchard). Stay tuned.

IOWA'S RIVERBOAT CASINOS

CASINO BELLE
Dubuque, Iowa
1-800-426-5591

Games: 500 Slot Machines, Blackjack, Craps, Roulette, Big 6
Schedule: 2 or 3 cruises a day of 4 to 5 hours each
Prices: $5 to $40 depending upon season, day of week, and whether or not the buffet is included
Opened: April, 1991

Location and Directions

The Casino Belle docks in Dubuque's Ice Harbor, and, while the boat is easy to locate when docked, finding the parking area and ticket booth can be tricky - especially at night.

No matter which route gets you to Dubuque (20, 52, 61, or 151), get onto Main Street and turn east on Third Street over the causeway to the Ice Harbor area. There you will find an Iowa Welcome Center, two floors of souvenir shops, and the Casino Belle ticket office. Parking is free, but you may end up 200 yards away because the Casino Belle has a capacity of 3000 passengers.

The Ice Harbor is also home to the Woodward Riverboat Museum and the Spirit of Dubuque, an excursion (non-gambling) paddlewheeler.

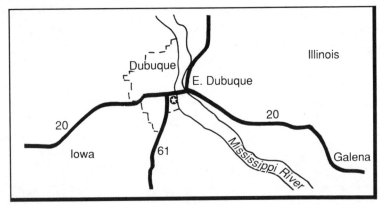

The Boat and Your Cruise

The Dubuque Casino Belle is a large boat. She has four decks containing three casino areas, two restaurants, a lounge, a children's activity area, and a gift shop.

When you make a reservation, you have an opportunity to get the buffet or not. Get the buffet. It features excellent prime rib along with the more traditional buffet fare. There is an ample salad bar and a good variety of entrees and side dishes along with tasty desserts. The only significant weakness is the vegetables; they are truly mediocre.

In the main restaurant area are a stage and a dance floor, and lounge acts perform during the evening cruises.

As the Iowa legislators probably intended, there does seem to be an honest effort to provide a variety of activities for adults and families. Although the casino tend to be the center of attraction, there are other reasons to take a cruise than to just gamble - as opposed to Illinois riverboats where your alternate activities are pretty much limited to watching the scenery and watching the people.

Local Sights and Entertainment

Dubuque, an attractive, river city of about 75,000, is 180 miles from Chicago and 105 miles from Madison, Wisconsin.

Visitors to the area can find a host of things to do before and after their riverboat ride. First, don't forget the Riverboat Museum right next to the Casino Belle. Downtown Dubuque has many antique and curio stores, and there is greyhound racing from April until November at Greyhound Park.

Five miles south of Dubuque is Crystal Lake Cave, a living cave with hundreds of beautiful formations. The 3/4 mile tour is only moderately rugged.

For more strenuous recreational activities, check out the Heritage Trail, a twenty-six mile trail along an abandoned railroad line. Hiking, biking, and cross-country skiing are available on this trail from Dubuque to Dyersville.

If that is too intimidating, just drive the twenty miles west on Route 20 to Dyersville to see the baseball diamond built in a corn field for the movie The Field of Dreams.

Just across the Mississippi and south ten miles in Galena, Illinois, you can tour U.S. Grant's home and shop the many antique shops in this historic town. Both Galena and Dubuque have downhill skiing available, although Chestnut Mountain (in Illinois) is a much larger ski area.

MISSISSIPPI BELLE II
Clinton, Iowa
1-800-457-9975

Games: 500 Slot Machines, Blackjack, Craps, Roulette
Schedule: 3 hour cruises, 3-5 each day
Price: $5 to $30, depending upon day, season, meal
Opened: April, 1991

Location and Directions

The Mississippi Belle II is the smallest of the 'first-generation' riverboat casinos. She was built in 1986 and operated as an excursion boat before being converted to a casino in 1990-91.

Take Route 30 or 67 to Clinton. The Mississippi Belle harbors at Showboat Landing, just off of Rt 67 two blocks north of Route 30. There is plenty of free parking. You purchase tickets at the City of Clinton Showboat, docked next door.

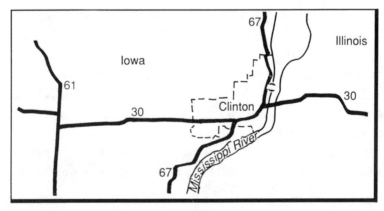

The Boat and Your Cruise

The Main Deck is a lounge and restaurant, while the Boiler Deck (second floor) contains the casino and a bar. One-half of the Texas Deck is a sandwich shop and souvenir store, and one-half is open air seating, and there is additional open deck space on the fourth level. This relatively large amount of open space reflects two things:

1. The Belle II's pedigree as a cruise boat.
2. Iowa's double standard that wants the gambling to attract visitors but doesn't really want them to gamble.

On weekends when the Mississippi Belle II is cruising (roughly April until October), she makes an 8 hour round trip from Clinton to Bellevue - about 35 miles each way. You can buy a ticket for the entire trip or for either half.

There is a 45 minute bus ride (cost $5) to take 'One-Way-ers' back to their origin. Cruises during the week and those in the evening are about 3 hours long and start and end in Clinton.

Local Sights and Entertainment

Other activities in the Clinton area are largely centered around the Mississippi River. Route 67 is a portion of The Great River Road, and there are often beautiful views of the river, bluffs, eagles, and the river bottom.

There are many antique shops along Clinton's main streets, and, if you check with the Tourist Bureau, you will find several delightful 'bed and breakfast' inns. William (Buffalo Bill) Cody's home is in LeClair, Iowa, twenty-three miles south of Clinton.

And from June through August, do not neglect the professional summer repertory at the City of Clinton Showboat, in permanent dry dock right next to the mooring of the Mississippi Belle II.

THE PRESIDENT RIVERBOAT CASINO
Davenport, Iowa
1-800-262-8711 (1-800-BOAT-711)

Games: Craps, Blackjack, Roulette, Big 6, 680 Slot Machines
Schedule: 4 cruises daily (3 on Sunday) about 4 hours each
Prices: $10 to $28 with food, $5 to $15 without
Opened: April, 1991

Location and Directions

"The Big One" is the self-awarded title of the President, and it is an apt appellation. Because of the 87-foot width and the 20-foot ceiling of the Main Deck, you get the feeling that you are in a large, land-based casino rather than on a riverboat.

The President has a capacity of 3000 passengers, and there seems to be room for all of them. The President makes her home at President's Landing in Davenport, just downstream of Centennial Bridge at the intersection of Routes 61 and 67 (directly across the river from the Casino Rock Island). There is plenty of parking.

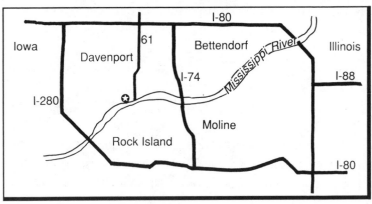

The Boat and Your Cruise

Of all the riverboat casinos, the President has the distinction of actually having a history as a riverboat. Most of the boats we've described here were newly built as riverboat casinos. The hull of the President was originally part of a side-wheeled, passenger steamboat, the Cincinnati, built in 1924. In 1932 she was removed from the overnight passenger business, stripped to the hull, rebuilt, and renamed the President. For almost 60 years, the President made excursion trips in St Louis and New Orleans until 1990 when she was outfitted as a casino and moved to the Quad Cities.

All of the fittings and decorations are new, but the President has logged many miles carrying lots of people on the Mississippi.

The food is good, quite good in fact, but the buffet line is so poorly lighted that you have to guess just what it is that you are serving yourself. The other flaw in the meal is that the desserts are amazingly small, not at all what one might hope for on the *Big One*.

The casino is spacious. There are 20 gaming tables on the main deck along with hundreds of Slot Machines, including 19 machines linked together to produce the largest Progressive jackpot so far on the Mississippi River. The choicest place to play the Slots or Blackjack is on the 2nd deck, which is actually a balcony overlooking the main casino. It's an impressive view and quite a contrast to the river scenery.

Local Sights and Entertainment

The sights and activities of the Quad Cities area have been covered before. From Davenport, all of these attractions are readily accessible. But there is one other event on the River that you will want to be aware of: eagle watching. From December through February, several hundred American Bald Eagles migrate to the Mississippi River between St Louis and Minneapolis.

Before or after your cruise on the President or any of the Mississippi River riverboats, drive along the Great River Road and look for these beautiful eagles resting in trees or soaring above the water seeking food. You can't miss the six-foot wing span, but take your binoculars and do not approach too close to the birds.

Several cities along the river organize eagle-sighting trips, and there are many marked lookout points from which to do your eagle watching. The first weekend in February is Bald Eagle Appreciation Days in the Quad Cities with assorted exhibits, lectures, and films about our national bird.

LOUISIANA'S RIVERBOAT CASINOS

Unfortunately, although the Louisiana legislature and governor have passed a law allowing riverboat casinos, there has yet to be any follow-up. Regulations have not been written, procedures have not been derived, and Louisiana is getting off to a slow start in this industry.

The latest estimate is that the first Louisiana riverboat casino will be launched in the Fall of 1993.

The Louisiana law allows no limit wagering and requires that all riverboat casinos be newly built (not converted from existing boats). This, combined with the fact that New Orleans is a major tourist and convention city already, should ensure that when the big wheels get rolling there should be some very nice boats coming onto the scene.

Watch for Bally's, Caesars World and Hilton to be among the established casino operators vying for a place in the New Orleans market. For now we will have to wait and see.

MISSISSIPPI'S RIVERBOAT CASINOS

In 1990 Mississippi passed legislation allowing counties along the Mississippi River and the Gulf Coast to vote on dockside casinos - the "boats" could be permanently docked. Nine counties have had referenda on the issue with six approving legalized gaming and three rejecting it.

Mississippi issued its first license for a riverboat casino in Natchez in November, 1991, but six months later, the license-holders canceled their plans. The first casino in Mississippi will open in the Summer of 1992 in Biloxi. It is not on a river, nor is it exactly a boat.

No other licenses have been issued by the state as of this writing, but several firms are planning operations in Mississippi.

THE ISLE OF CAPRI CASINO
Biloxi, Mississippi
1-800-843-4753 (1-800-THE-ISLE)

Games: 600 Slot Machine, Blackjack, Craps, Big 6 upon opening: Mini-Baccarat and Roulette to follow
Schedule: permanently docked, no cruises; open 24 hours
Price: No admission charge
Opened: August, 1992

Location and Directions

As you drive along Rt 90, you will find The Isle of Capri Casino at 151 Beach Blvd, just west of I-110. On land is a large building containing the ticket booths, a restaurant, and the inevitable souvenir shop. The casino is actually two boats that are newly relocated to the Gulf and do not move from their new, permanent moorings.

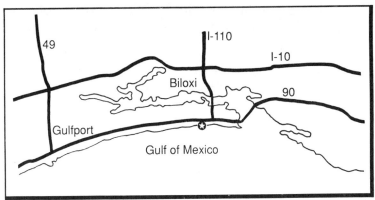

The Boat and Your Cruise

During the first year that the riverboat casinos were legal, five riverboats cruised in Iowa. As "no limit" casinos opened in Illinois, more and more competition developed for the local pool of gamblers, and the Iowa boats found it hard to compete against the higher betting limits available on the other side of the river.

After that first year, the owners of two of the Iowa riverboats decided to move them to the State of Mississippi where they would not be subject to the betting limitations of Iowa.

The Diamond Lady and The Emerald Lady toured the Mississippi River in Iowa through the first part of July, 1992, then started their move down the river to Biloxi. They are scheduled to open as The Isle of Capri on August 1, 1992.

For the first three months that the casino is open, the boats will be remodeled extensively to adapt to their new home. The on-board restaurants, shops, and lounges will be removed and the casino areas will expand into these decks. More Slot Machines will be added as well and Mini-Baccarat and Roulette and additional tables of Black-jack and Craps.

It is reported that someone who visited the "old" Diamond Lady or Emerald Lady will not recognize them after the make-over is finished.

Local Sights and Entertainment

Biloxi is a part of the Old South while thriving in the high technology of the Space Age. It is a combination resort city and major port on the Gulf of Mexico.

Tourists to Biloxi are likely to center their activities on the 26-mile, white sand Mississippi Beach. Swim, sail, fish, or cruise. You can even take a trip on board an authentic shrimp trawler. You will also find a full range of theme, amusement, and water parks.

But don't neglect some of the other activities that Biloxi provides. History buffs should see Beauvoir, the last home of Jefferson Davis, President of the Confederacy. The site includes two museums and many beautiful artifacts.

Or check out the Old Spanish Fort about 25 miles east in Pascagoula. The fort was built in 1718 and is believed to be the oldest structure in the entire central portion of the United States.

About 25 miles west of Biloxi is the Stennis Space Center, where shuttle craft engines are tested before launch. There is a variety of activities for astronauts-to-be of all ages.

And if you can't get enough gambling aboard The Isle of Capri, you may want to book a trip aboard La Cruise for a daytime or evening cruise. La Cruise offers food, live entertainment, and - once she gets into international waters - a full range of casino gambling.

If you are in Biloxi the first weekend of June, be sure to attend the Shrimp Festival - Fais Do Do, and see the decorated shrimp fleet parade through the Biloxi Harbor. And in September, watch for the world's largest Sand Sculpture Contest. You'll never forget it.

LADY LUCK NATCHEZ
Natchez, Mississippi

Games: Slot Machines, Craps, Blackjack, Big 6, Roulette
Schedule: none - permanently docked structure
Prices: Not determined yet
Opened: Scheduled for October, 1992

Location and Directions

This riverboat casino will be owned and operated by the company that owns the Lady Luck Casino in Las Vegas. At the Natchez-Vidalia Bridge (Rts 65 and 84) exit on Canal Street and follow the signs to the Natchez Under-the-Hill historic district.

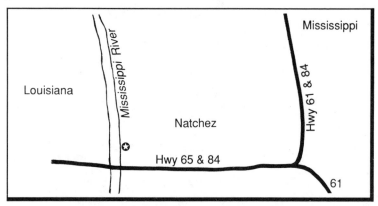

Local Sights and Entertainment

The city of Natchez has been a city much longer than the United States has been a country. Evidence shows the Natchez (Creek) Indians lived here for generations before LaSalle 'discovered' the city in 1662. It was the capital of Mississippi for two short periods around the beginning of the nineteenth century, and was a thriving mercantile port during the era of the steamboats.

When you visit Natchez today, you owe it to yourself to explore at least two facets of the history of the area. First, there is the Natchez Trace, the remnants of a 450-mile wilderness road from Nashville to Natchez. Originally an Indian route, the Trace was cleared during the early 1800's for use by traders, soldiers, settlers and missionaries.

The advent of the steamboats led to the decline of the Natchez Trace as a major artery, but there is a lot of history along its route. Within twenty miles of Natchez, you can see Mount Locust, one of the earliest inns along the Trace (restored), Indian mounds, and traces of the old Trace roadway. Don't miss it.

The other wonder of Natchez is its stunning array of antebellum homes. At least forty major historic homes are available for tours, some year-round and some during the Spring (March) and Fall (October) Pilgrimages. If you've wondered about life at Tara, here is your chance to get a taste.

And after you have had your fill of history, stop off at the restaurants and bars of Natchez Under-the-Hill, the riverfront site of the old ferry landing, now a day-and-night hot spot.

MISSISSIPPI'S OTHER RIVERBOATS

Between the time I am writing this and the time you are reading it, the riverboat casino situation in Mississippi has probably changed. Look for casinos in Gulfport on the Gulf of Mexico and in the northwest corner of the state, near Memphis, Tennessee.

There is also serious interest in a second riverboat casino in Natchez. You should call the Mississippi Department of Tourism for current information on other riverboats in the state.

Steamin' Along

IV. CASINO GAMES SECTION

INTRODUCTION

Today's riverboat casinos offer a selection of games that is similar to what you will find in the casinos of Nevada or Atlantic City: Blackjack, Craps, Slot Machines, Video Poker, Roulette, Baccarat, and Big 6.

We will go through each of these games, explain the rules and procedures, and present some of the basic strategies to minimize the House's odds and show you how to be a winner.

You will be more comfortable entering a game if you know what the rules are and what is expected, and your odds of winning are enhanced if you take the time to learn what bets to avoid and what playing strategy to use. Even the occasional traveler to Atlantic City or Las Vegas may want to review this section for we cover the rules, options and winning strategies there as well.

Gamblers offer a variety of reasons why they gamble: some like the excitement, some mention the entertainment, for some it is the challenge. But the heart of the matter is the money.

The pleasure you derive from gambling is going to be vastly greater if you take a cruise on one of the riverboats and leave the boat a winner. It is not enough merely to know all of the odds and betting strategies for the games presented here, you have to learn the techniques of good money management.

Money management is the secret to cutting your losses when you are losing, and it is the way to escalate your winnings to possibly turn a successful session into a truly memorable one. So, let's start with a discussion on managing your money.

MONEY MANAGEMENT

The games on the riverboats and all other casinos are carefully designed so that the House has an expected edge over the average player. If you play any of their games for any length of time, the most likely outcome is that you will lose money - if you are an average player.

And except for Blackjack, each event in casino games, each roll of the dice or spin of the wheel, is an independent occurrence - the result of the last turn has no effect on what will happen next. Just because red came up last time does not make it any more or less likely that black will come up the next time.

While it is not likely, it is entirely possible for you to sit down at Roulette, bet on red all night long, and win with every spin of the wheel. In the short run, anything can happen. Over enough time though, the outcome of each of these games will approach the percentages that are discussed in this book.

Certainly, many passengers will win. Some will be lucky; they will drop a quarter in a slot machine and win a jackpot of $500 or more. Some will be more than lucky; they will have learned the games and know which bets to make and which to avoid, and they will know the strategies to help them literally beat the House at its own game.

This book will show you exactly these things. The pages which follow will help you be a winner.

No doubt about it, everyone wants to be a winner, but you must consider the possiblility that on any given cruise you might not win. The very first rule of money management is to be prepared for the worst.

Before you step foot on a riverboat, you should know exactly how much you are willing loose. Clearly your answer to this question depends on your present financial status, your continuing income, and your tolerance of risk.

One person might react to the loss of $1000 just as easily as another would to the loss of $10. Your answer depends on you - and to an extent on the riverboat you are going to ride - as noted, Iowa has a $200 limit on an individual's loss on a single cruise.

You should then consider that sum of money, not as an abstract possible loss, but as a very real stack of one dollar bills sitting in front of you.

Assume your maximum loss amount is $100. Can you afford to do without that $100? It is very easy to picture what to do with the money that you intend to win! But remember: you must anticipate the possibility that you are going to lose.

If the $100 were to disappear, would it be tougher to pay the bills near the end of the month? Would you have to put off getting the car fixed? Would the insurance payment have to wait a few days longer?

If the $100 represents any of these things, then you need to reconsider the amount that you are willing to gamble. Perhaps your limit should be $50 or $20 or $0.

Do not gamble with money that you cannot afford to lose.

Let's assume that you have determined that $100 is the total amount that you are willing to risk on your cruise. The next step is to determine how much to wager on each bet, how much your 'unit' bet will be. Each of the games you participate in will have swings both for and against you.

Much of the time, your wins and losses will tend to pretty much alternate, then, all of a sudden, you win eight bets in a row or lose ten bets in a row.

If your unit bet is too large in relation to your $100 total stake, you may be wiped out by a swing that goes against you before you have the chance to capitalize on a swing in your favor.

The rule of thumb is that your unit should be about one-fortieth of your total stake. If your stake is $100, your usual bet should be $2.50 to provide you enough of a cushion to ride out an adverse swing. It may not seem like much, but do not worry, you will have plenty of action. If your stake is $1000, you can prudently bet in the $25 range.

And for the other side of the coin: how high is up? Each of us would like to win it all. The fact is though, that the more you try to win it all, the more opportunity you are giving the House to get back the money you have already won. Even when you are winning, you have to keep firmly in mind your loss limit.

As you start to win, if you feel comfortable with larger bets, increase your unit bet to one-fortieth of your new total stake. For instance, if you work your $100 bankroll up to $120, you are safe raising your average bet up to $3.

When you get up enough that you are ahead one-half of your original stake, start to set aside money that you won't touch no matter what. Put $50 away. Put it in your pocket. And adjust your mental picture so that you still have $100 - not $150 - at risk.

At this point, if you are cautious, drop your unit bet back to $2.50 to reflect the size of your new stake. If you are more adventuresome, raise your average bet to $4, which is the correct unit for a bankroll of $150, even though you are only playing with $100.

If you keep winning and you are ahead by an amount equal to your original bankroll, it is time to take stock. You have had a good session, you have beaten the House, and you may want to quit a quaranteed winner.

Or if you have the temperament that I do, you may want to continue playing and try for a truly big win, one that you can brag about when you get back home. In this case, keep setting money aside so that you have no more than your original stake at risk, but continue to increase your bet so that it represents about one-fortieth of your total stake plus winnings.

If your stake was $100 and you double that, put $100 away and start making $5 bets (1/40 of $200). As you win, continue to increase your bets appropriately.

If the tide turns against you and you lose the $100 you have on the table, stop. DO NOT TOUCH THE MONEY THAT YOU HAVE PUT ASIDE. Your ability to control yourself and walk away with the casino's money is what will truly make you a winner.

By using good money management, you are not likely to get rich from the casinos. But you are not going to get burned too badly either.

The average passenger on the riverboats loses between $50 and $60. That is not too high a price to pay for the entertainment if you can afford it, but think how mucn more exciting it would be to go on a 3-hour cruise and win $50.

Smart money management and smart playing will help you do exactly that.

CASINO BASICS

If you have never entered a casino, you will find that a whole new world awaits you there. Even the smallest of the riverboat casinos has hundreds of thousands of dollars invested in the colorful, glittering Slot Machines. There is a well-trained staff of dozens of employees who are eager to help you participate in the games offered.

At even a $2 Blackjack table, there will be a rack containing chips with a total value of thousands of dollars. You should be impressed with all of the money, time, and effort that has gone into the layout of the casino, but do not be overwhelmed by it all. If you put a quarter in a Slot Machine or place a $500 bet at the Craps table, it is your money you are gambling with.

Keep a clear head, and always make the bets that give you the best chance of winning at the game of your choice.

In the discussion which follows, we will cover each of the bets that are available on every game on every riverboat now in operation.

Understanding Payoffs

At all of the games available in the casino, the payoff for a bet is expressed in terms of that bet. For instance, if you bet on a single number at Roulette and that number wins, you are paid at the rate of 35 to 1. This means that you will end up with your original bet plus winnings of 35 times that bet, a total of 36 times your bet.

At the Slot Machines and sometimes at the table games, odds will be given as, for example, 5 for 1. If you win a bet of this sort, you will only end up with 5 times your original bet, not 6 times.

In general, odds of 2 for 1 are the same as odds of 1 to 1. This difference is important to remember in the discussion below and when you're considering which game to play and which bets to make.

Chip Denominations

In the riverboat casinos, bets at the table games are made with plastic chips which come in a variety of denominations, differentiated by color.

The most commonly used chips are:

Riverboat Chip Denominations	
$1	white
$2.50	pink
$5	red
$25	green
$100	black

Chips and Tokens

Chips are available at the **cashier's cage** or you may purchase them at the table by placing your cash on the playing surface about halfway between you and the Dealer before the start of any hand. Any chips you have when you leave a game must be redeemed at the cashier.

The Slot Machines use metal tokens to represent twenty-five cent, dollar, and five dollar bets. There will be **Change Booths** near the Slot Machine areas where you can acquire tokens before you start to play the Slots.

You will also see Change Girls moving among the machines selling tokens. Any tokens that you wish to convert back to cash must be taken to the Change Booth.

Dealing With Mistakes

The casino staff is highly trained and there are Pit Bosses who try to keep an eagle eye on every move at every game, but all of these people are human and mistakes do occur.

If you feel that a mistake has occurred against you, speak up politely but immediately. Perhaps a bet that should have been a winner was collected by the Dealer. Perhaps you received the incorrect number of chips in exchange for cash or chips. Whatever.

If you feel that a mistake has cost you money, speak up. The situation will be dealt with and corrected. If you wait even a few seconds, it may be too late for the staff to reconstruct what happened, and you are less likely to be happy with the final result.

If a mistake happens in your favor, the issue is between you and your conscience. Some Players feel compelled to point out the mistake and get it corrected even though it costs them. Some take the attitude that the House determined all of the rules in the game, and this must just be a rule that the Player was not aware of; they accept the windfall without speaking up.

I am not going to advise you one way or the other except for one special case: if you like your teeth where they are, do not point out a mistake that occurred in another Player's favor.

Iowa Gambling Limit

All of the casinos in Iowa are bound by the $200 limitation of losses by an individual on a cruise. This is monitored fairly smoothly by the issuance of coupons or *scrip* in the value of $200 when you purchase your ticket.

On the riverboat, when you wish to buy chips or tokens, you must exchange both cash and an equivalent amount of scrip for the chips. After you have purchased $200 worth of chips, you are out of scrip and are ineligible to buy any more during that cruise.

Although this complies with the technical requirements of the Iowa laws, you will find that it is very easy to locate fellow passengers who are not going to use all of their allotment of scrip and who will buy chips or tokens for you.

Iowa Betting Limits

In the casino, betting is restricted to the limits proscribed by Iowa's legislation. The maximum bet that you can place is $5. Therefore, you will find generally 2 types of tables: those that allow a betting range of $3 to $5 and those that allow bets of $5. This is common to all of the Iowa riverboats.

Interestingly, the law does allow you to play more than one hand at a time, though the casino personnel may restrict your option to do this when the casino is busy. Also, if the Blackjack table is full, you can place a bet on another person's hand.

Thus, if you were really determined to bet more than the posted limit, you and a friend could sit down at a full Blackjack table, each bet $5 on your own hand and each bet $5 on each other's hand. In effect, you would be betting $10 on each hand (as long as you and your friend could keep the accounting straight).

The Craps and Roulette are generally $3 to $5. At these games, if you want to exceed the $5 per bet limit, you have to have one or more non-gambling friends play along side you and make the same bets that you do.

A Note About Smoking

A very unscientific survey concludes that a relatively large percentage of gamblers smoke. The casinos are aware of this and ashtrays are provided at the tables and alongside the Slot Machines.

Each of the riverboats also has designated non-smoking tables. There are no non-smoking areas in the Slot Machine pits. It is my experience that, if the non-smoking seats are mostly filled, the casino personnel are generally willing to designate a table as non-smoking if there is a unanimous request from the players seated there. Don't be afraid to ask.

And now, let's look at the games offered by the riverboat casinos.

WINNING AT BLACKJACK

Blackjack or **Twenty-one** is the most popular of the table games in the United States. It is fast - a hand takes from fifteen to ninety seconds. It is fair - playing the Basic Strategy you will learn here, you are playing almost even with the House. And it is fun.

Blackjack is one of the two games on the riverboats in which your play can affect the outcome; you are not just waiting for the ball to fall or the dice to roll, you choose to take the next card or not.

Blackjack is played with a standard deck of 52 cards. An Ace counts as either 1 or 11, the cards Two through Ten count as their face value, and the **face cards** (Jack, Queen, and King) count as 10. In Blackjack, the suits have no significance.

The casinos generally use six decks of cards shuffled together to make one massive stack of over 300 cards. The reasons for this are that it gives the House a slightly higher edge measured in hundredths of a percent, it discourages card counting (more about that later), and it speeds up the game because the Dealer does not have to shuffle as often.

Object of the Game

Each player plays separately against the House, represented by the Dealer. The object is to beat the Dealer by getting cards totaling close to 21 without going bust, exceeding 21.

The Player wins if his total is 21 or less and either:
• It is higher than the Dealer's total, or
• The Dealer busts.

The Player loses if he
• Busts, or
• Has a total that is less than the Dealer's and the Dealer does not bust.

Any time both the Player and the Dealer have the same hand of 21 or less, it is a tie, called a **push**, and no one wins or loses.

The Table and How to Play

The Blackjack table is roughly semi-circular in shape. The Dealer stands behind the flat side, and the Players sit along the curved edge. In front of the Dealer is a built-in rack for chips that is the bank for the House. To the Dealer's left is the **shoe**, a tilted box that holds the cards after they are shuffled prior to being dealt. To the Dealer's right is a **discard rack** where cards that have been played are kept until it is time to shuffle again.

The Blackjack Layout

Blackjack
Pays 3 to 2

Dealer must draw to 16 and stand on all 17s

Insurance pays 2 to 1

Printed on the felt, you will see six or seven circles to denote the location of the player's bets and two rules which serve to mark the location where cards are played.

Also on the table somewhere will be a small sign indicating the range of bets that are accepted at the table. For example, a table might allow bets of $3-$5 or $5-$1000. Each Player must bet at least the minimum posted for the table on each hand.

If there is a Player's circle available and you are willing to wager at least the minimum for the table, you may join in the game. To bet, place your wager in the empty circle in front of you. If you are betting more than one chip, stack them neatly.

If you are betting more than one denomination of chip, arrange them in ascending order top to bottom. That is, if you wish to bet $7 with a $5 chip and two $1 chips, put all three chips in one stack with the $5 chip on the bottom.

The Play of the Game

When all Players have placed their bets, the Dealer starts the deal by placing a card face-up in front of each bet on the table, working clockwise around the table. His own card will be placed face-down. Then the Dealer will give each Player a second card, also face-up. He will deal his own second card face-down and then turn over his first card.

At this point you will be able to see both of your cards and all of the cards of each of the other Players and one card of the Dealer's.

The Dealer can also see both of your cards, but that doesn't matter because his decisions are completely controlled by his cards, not by yours. You, the Player, are the only one who has a choice of the plays that you may want to make.

When it is your turn to play, you can choose to take a card or to stand based on the total of the cards that you have in your hand and on the Dealer's card that is visible.

In your hand, an Ace can count as 1 or 11. If your hand either has no Aces or the Aces are counted as 1's, you have a hard hand. For instance, Ten-Six-Ace is a *hard 17*. A hand with an Ace counted as

11 is a **soft** hand; an Ace-Six is a *soft 17*.

If the Dealer does not have an Ace showing, he will start with the Player to his left and offer each player an opportunity to play out his hand. To avoid confusion and to leave a clear trail on the monitors videotaping the games, all responses are made by hand signal instead of verbally. The Dealer will point to each hand in turn and wait for the Player's response.

If you wish to **hit**, that is receive another card, you lightly scratch the tabletop toward y1ou with your fingertips or point toward your cards with your index finger.

Based on your card total and the Dealer's upcard, you may want to take several cards until you either reach a point total where you want to stay or you bust. If you want to stand - refuse additional cards, wave your hand sideways palm down across your bet.

Try to make clear, unambiguous hand signals. If unsure, most Dealers will ask you what you meant, but if you are unclear, you may end up with a card that you did not really want or the Player to your left will receive a card that you did intend to ask for. Either way, when you make plays that are not optimum, you are reducing your chances of winning.

In a situation where the House has defined all of the rules, you do not want to do anything that will limit the effectiveness of the choices that you do have. A Player who makes clear hand signals makes the game more pleasant for himself and his fellow Players.

As a rule, the Dealer is on your side in any of the casino games. He will not cheat to help you win, but he may offer advice and will certainly answer politely phrased questions. Two reasons for this is that the Dealer is doing his job and his eight hour shift will pass more quickly if he is having fun, and a significant portion of a Dealer's income comes from tips, and happy, winning Players tip more than grumpy, losing ones.

If you take too many cards and end up with a total that is greater than 21, you lose immediately. The Dealer will scoop up your cards and your wager before proceeding to the next Player. When each of the Players has had an opportunity to play, the Dealer will turn up his hole card and play his own hand.

The Dealer's play is completely pre-determined. He must take a card if his total is less than 17, and stand if his total is 17 or greater. In a Player's hand, an Ace can count as either one or eleven, but in the Dealer's hand, an Ace must be an eleven unless his total would be greater than 21, in which case an Ace is counted as one.

This means that if the Dealer has an Ace and a Six, he must count the Ace as 11 so his total is a "soft" 17 and he must stand with that hand. This is true even if it were the case that he could look at each of the players hands and see that everyone else has a 20.

On some of the riverboats, the Dealer must hit a soft 17. One of the two rules printed on the felt of the tabletop covers this situation. It will either say that the Dealer stands on all 17's or that the Dealer must hit a soft 17.

Hitting soft 17 provides a slight additional edge to the House, but does not change the fact that the Dealer has a rigid set of requirements that he must follow in playing his hand.

The Dealer will continue to take cards until his total is 17 or greater. If he busts, then all of the Players who are still in the game and did not bust earlier are paid. If he gets to a total between 17 and 21, that total is compared to each Player's total.

Players with higher totals than the deler win, lower totals lose, and ties, called **pushes**, are neither paid nor forfeited.

On almost every hand, you have the opportunity to either stand or take one or more hits. There are additional options that may be available to Players:

Insurance

If the Dealer's up card is an Ace, each Player may place an insurance bet. You may bet any amount, up to one-half of your original wager, that the value of the Dealer's down card is ten. The chips representing an insurance bet are placed just outside your circle toward the Dealer.

If the Dealer's down card is a **10-card** (a Ten or a face card), all insurance bets are paid at the rate of 2 to 1. That is, you win $2 for each

$1 that you bet on insurance.

If the Dealer's down card has any other value than 10, your insurance bet loses and is collected immediately. After the insurance bet is settled, your original bet and hand are played normally. If the Dealer's down card is a 10-card in these circumstances, it means that he has Blackjack, an automatic winner unless a Player also has Blackjack.

Insurance bets are only offered when the Dealer has an Ace showing, but the Dealer also may have a Blackjack when he has a 10-card showing. On the riverboats and in most casinos, if the Dealer is showing a 10-card, he will immediately check the down card to see if it is an Ace, and if it is, he will turn the Ace over right away and collect all of the bets except from any Players who also have Blackjack.

You will notice in some casinos, the Dealer will not check his down card until all of the Players have played out their hands. Where this rule is in effect, the casinos handle things so that the result is the same for the Player as if the Dealer had looked first.

If a Player has split a pair and/or doubled down during the play of his hand, the Dealer will only collect one losing wager from that hand - the other bets still belong to the Player.

Doubling Down

You have the option of increasing your wager on a hand by **doubling down** on the first two cards you receive. You signal your intention of doubling down by placing a stack of chips equal to your original bet along-side it in your betting circle.

Technically you can double down for less than your original bet, but in reality you want to increase your bet as much as possible because you will be doubling down when there is a higher probability that you will win.

The Dealer will give you exactly one more card and those three cards will determine your total for that hand. If you win, you will get paid an amount equal to the sum of your two stacks of chips. If you lose, you lose both bets, and it is not a pretty sight.

Splitting Pairs

If your first 2 cards have the same value, you may **split** them into two hands and play each one separately. This is indicated by placing an equal stack of chips next to your original bet. Do not touch the cards.

The Dealer will give a second card for the first hand, and you play it out until you bust or stand. Then you will get a second card on the second hand and play out that hand. If the second card on either hand is the same value as the first, you may choose to split again. Most casinos allow you to split until you have four hands.

You may also double down on the first two cards of part of a split hand. That is, if you split Six's and got a Five on the first Six, your total for that hand would be 11. You may double down on the 11 if you wish, and would receive exactly one more card on that hand. Then you'll receive a second card to the second six and have the option to stand or hit.

On at least two of the riverboat casinos, you cannot double down after you split a pair. When you sit at a Blackjack table, ask specifically about this rule as it will affect your playing strategy.

You can split a Ten and a face card since they both have a value of 10. As we'll discuss later, unless you're a card counter, you should never make such a play, though it's legal and you'll see players do it.

If your first two cards are Aces and you split them, you will get only one more card on each Ace.

Surrender

If the Dealer does not have Blackjack, you may **surrender** your hand before you have taken a third card. This is the one play that is done verbally. Do not make a hand signal; just say Surrender. The Dealer will take one half of your bet and pick up your cards. In effect you have forfeited one half of your bet and not played out the hand.

This option is not available on riverboats operating now, but it is available in several casinos in Las Vegas and Atlantic City and is described here for it may be offered in the future.

The Blackjack

There is one other element to the game of Blackjack, the Blackjack itself. If your first two cards in either order are an Ace and a 10-card, you have a Blackjack. If the Dealer does not have a Blackjack also, you win one and one-half times your wager, for example a $5 bet will win $7.50.

If the Dealer also has a Blackjack you push. The House automatically beats any other Players who do not have Blackjacks. If you split a pair of Aces and get a 10-card on either of them, that hand is not a Blackjack since it was not your first two cards. It is a 21, a very good hand, but it can be beaten if the Dealer has a Blackjack.

Table Etiquette Reviewed

Once the Dealer has finished playing his hand and settled the wagers for each of the Players, he will collect up all of the cards and put them in the discard stack. At this time you should be preparing your wager for the next hand, so that when the Dealer is ready so are you.

Let's have a quick review of the table etiquette:

• To indicate that you want to play a hand, place your chip(s) neatly in the empty circle in front of you arranged in increasing value. If you want to get change, put your chips OUTSIDE of the circle and ask the Dealer for change.

• Do not touch the cards.

• If the Dealer has an Ace up, he will ask if you want to place an insurance bet. If you do, it goes outside the circle toward the Dealer.

• To take a hit, scratch lightly toward you or point to your cards with your index finger

• To stand, wave sideways palm down,

• To split or double down, place an amount equal to your original wager next to - not on - your first stack of chips. Almost always it will be clear which you want to do; if it is not, the Dealer will ask.

There is one other etiquette point that should be made. At the Blackjack table, and at no other gambling game that I've been involved in, it is all too common for ill-mannered, and generally ill-informed, players to make negative comments on another Player's style of play.

When you place your chips in your circle, you are paying for the right to play your cards exactly as you wish within the rules of the casino. If a fellow Player does not like the play you make and chooses to comment on it, do not change your style just to please the crowd. It is your money; you owe it to yourself to play the game to the best of your ability.

By the same token, do not comment on the play of another. If you take the time to learn the strategy presented here, you will be the best player at your table, but each of the others is playing with his own money and is entitled to make his own choices.

You will get more enjoyment from your session at the table if you ignore the rude comments of others and do not contribute any yourself.

It will happen, though, that sometimes a neighboring Player will ask you which play he should make. I find it safest to hedge a little and say something like, *Well, the book says that you should take a hit.*

You don't want to gain an enemy by recommending the correct action that happens not to work that particular hand. Offer the correct advice if you are sure that you know it, and let the player make his own decision.

Thoughts About Strategy

Unless the dealer has a Blackjack and you lose automatically, you will have an opportunity on every hand to directly affect the outcome of the hand. By making the optimum choice at these times, your odds are almost exactly even with the House, and you can actually have a winning edge by moving on and learning a non-counting or counting strategy.

Fortunately for the casinos, most players do not invest the hour or two required to understand and practice the optimum strategy.

At this point, some of you are asking, "Why does the House have an edge at all? A push is a tie; the Player can decide whether or not to take an additional card while the Dealer is restricted in his play; a

Blackjack for the Player pays 3 to 2, but a Blackjack for the Dealer only costs the Player his original bet. Where does the House have any advantage in the game?"

The answer is that the House has a huge advantage because the Player goes first. If the Player busts, he loses even if the Dealer busts a few seconds later. This simple rule is enough to allow the House to offer you such options as doubling down, 3 to 2 for Blackjack, etc.

But now someone is thinking, "Ah ha! I'll fool them. I'll never take a card that will allow me to bust. I'll stand whenever I have 12 or more, and the House will lose that edge."

Trust me; if it were that easy, there would be a rule against it. In order to maximize your chances of winning, there are times that you 'must' take a card even though you know that the odds are high that you will bust.

Winning With Card Counting

One more side issue: card counting. Once a hand of Blackjack is completed, the cards dealt for it are stacked in the discard rack and are not used again until the deck is shuffled. Thus, the next hand depends somewhat on the hands that preceeded it.

There are proven techniques to allow the Player to keep track of the cards that have been played and to alter his bet and playing strategy to take advantage of situations where the remaining cards are favorable for the Player.

It is beyond the scope of this book to get into the specifics of card counting, and I recommend that you don't worry about it for now. If you read the following section carefully, get a deck of cards and practice and learn the strategy presented here, you will be on an almost even footing with the casino.

In a two to four hour cruise, you have a very real opportunity to come out ahead even if you sit down at the first hand and play until the boat docks.

When you have mastered this strategy, if you have an inclination toward numbers and would like to explore card counting, there are some excellent advanced strategies on the subject listed at the end of this book. Get one of these and work on the simple counting techniques that will give you a mathematical edge and the expectancy at winning.

I have counted cards. It can be profitable, but I found that it removes a large portion of the enjoyment from the game because it is so much work. I have friends who count regularly and swear by it, but you do not need it to enjoy the game.

WARNING: Casinos consider card counting to be illegal. They can legally bar you from playing Blackjack if they suspect that you are counting down the deck.

The Basic Strategy

In a standard six-deck shoe, there are 24 Aces, 96 10-cards, and 192 other cards (Twos through Nines) for a total of 312 cards.

Remember, the suits do not matter, just the value of the cards. When it is your turn to make a decision about your hand, you have two pieces of information available to you: the current total of your hand and the Dealer's up card.

Because almost one-third of the cards are 10-cards, one assumption that you will make is that any card you cannot see, including the Dealer's down card and the next card to be dealt, is a 10-card.

Thus, if the Dealer's up card is a Four, the Basic Strategy presumes that the Dealer's hand totals 14 because the Dealer's down card is more likely to be a 10 than any other value. By the same token, if you take a hit, that card is most likely going to be a 10-card.

Your first question should be: do I have a **pat hand**, a hand that totals 17 or more and does not include any Aces counted as 11? Examples of pat hands would be Ten and Queen (20) or Jack and Eight (18) A hand that consists of an Ace and a Seven (8 or 18) is not a pat hand.

If your answer is 'Yes', you do have a pat hand, you should never take a card. With a pat hand, your response is always to make the sideways wave of your hand indicating that you want to stand. In short, never hit a hard 17 or higher.

There is one exception to this rule. If you have a pair of Nines

64

(totalling 18), there will be times that you should split them and play two hands. Otherwise the rule stands: if you have a pat hand, stand.

Second question: is my total 8 or less? If the cards in your hand are so small that your total is smaller than 9, you will always - ALWAYS - take a card. At least one. It doesn't depend on what the Dealer has showing, you will scratch the felt indicating that you want a hit (unless you have a pair of Two's, Three's or Four's, in which case you might split them as we will soon see.)

What could be easier? If you have a really high hand, one that totals to 17 or more when you count the Aces as 1, you don't take any more cards. If you have a really low hand with no Aces, a total of 8 or less, not a pair, you always take at least one card.

A few more *always* and *never* rules:

Always Split Aces
An Ace is the strongest first card you can have for a hand, and by splitting a pair of them, you start out with two strong hands.

Always Split Eights
Two eights total 16 which is trouble for the Player. But if the Dealer has a low card showing, you have a good chance to make two good hands and win both of them. If the Dealer has a good, high card exposed, you are trying to get one good hand so that you win one and perhaps push the other.

Leaving the Eights together to make 16, you are either counting on the Dealer to bust or you are going to take a hit in a situation where only five of the thirteen possible cards (Ace through Five, not Six through King) will help you. There are times that you will hit a 16 but if your 16 is made up of two Eights, split 'em up.

Never Split Fives or 10-cards
You will never get enough 20's; don't go throwing them away by splitting up your Tens. The situation with two Fives is similar. A total of 10 is a great start to a hand, while a 5 is a miserable start.

It is by winning your splits and double downs that you will win at a session of Blackjack, but that should not drive you to folly. Keep your 20's and play your two Fives as 10's. Forget that they are a pair of Fives.

Never Hit an Ace-Eight Or An Ace-Nine

The same applies to other combination of cards that totals Ace-Eight or Ace-Nine, like Ace-Three - Five. These are soft hands that qualify as pat hands; they are quite good, and the odds are that you will only make them worse if you take a hit or double down.

Never Make An Insurance Bet

You will recall that you can place an Insurance bet when the dealer has an Ace showing. An Insurance bet wins $2 for each $1 bet if the Dealer's down card is a 10-card, otherwise the Player loses his Insurance bet.

Since there are thirteen possible down cards, and four of them are 10-cards, the odds against an Insurance bet winning are 9 to 4 (or 2.25 to 1). But the pay-off is only 8 to 4 (2 to 1). The difference, 8%, is the edge that goes to the house.

Do not place Insurance bets unless you are counting cards and know that the number of 10-cards is more than one-third of the total number of cards remaining in the shoe.

This rule is true even if you have a Blackjack. There are Players - many of them - who will tell you that insuring a Blackjack is a sure thing. Either you will win the Insurance bet if the Dealer has a Blackjack or you will win the hand if he doesn't. True enough.

If you are going to play exactly one hand, and you get a Blackjack and the Dealer exposes an Ace, take Insurance and walk away with some winnings.

But if you are going to continue to play, save your Insurance bets. They work in the favor of the House, and you are likely to be better off at the end of the cruise if you do not ever place an Insurance bet.

These are all of the rules that depend only on the cards in your hand. In every other situation, your action depends on your total and what the Dealer has showing.

Optimum Basic Strategy for Multiple Deck Blackjack
Initial Two Card Total
Double Down After Split Allowed

YOUR HAND	DEALER'S				UPCARD					
	2	3	4	5	6	7	8	9	10	A
5-8	H	H	H	H	H	H	H	H	H	H
9	H	D	D	D	D	H	H	H	H	H
10	D	D	D	D	D	D	D	D	H	H
11	D	D	D	D	D	D	D	D	D	H
12	H	H	S	S	S	H	H	H	H	H
13-16	S	S	S	S	S	H	H	H	H	H
A2-A3	H	H	H	D	D	H	H	H	H	H
A4-A5	H	H	D	D	D	H	H	H	H	H
A6	H	D	D	D	D	H	H	H	H	H
A7	S	D	D	D	D	S	S	H	H	H
A8-A9	S	S	S	S	S	S	S	S	S	S
A-10			-----	BLACKJACK			-----			
AA	spl	spl	spl	spl	spl	spl	spl	spl	spl	spl
22-33	spl	spl	spl	spl	spl	spl	H	H	H	H
44	H	H	H	spl	spl	H	H	H	H	H
55	D	D	D	D	D	D	D	D	H	H
66	spl	spl	spl	spl	spl	H	H	H	H	H
77	spl	spl	spl	spl	spl	spl	H	H	H	H
88	spl	spl	spl	spl	spl	spl	spl	spl	spl	spl
99	spl	spl	spl	spl	spl	S	spl	spl	S	S
10-10	S	S	S	S	S	S	S	S	S	S

H = Hit   **S** = Stand   **D** = Double   **spl** = Split
Do not split 5-5 and 10-10. Always split A-A and 8-8.

Playable and Stiff Totals

If your hand does not fit into one of the situations above, then it is either *playable*, has a hard total of 11 or less, or is a *stiff*, with a total of 12 to 16. Your actions depend upon the Dealer's up card.

Generally you will make your decision based on whether the Dealer's up card is 6 or less or is 7 or greater. If you will look at the strategy chart, you will notice that on many of the lines across the page, the action that the Player takes changes as the Dealers card switches from a Six to a Seven.

We are going to look at the situations one at a time working our way down the chart. Let's start with *hard* hands - hands with no Aces:

You Have Two Cards That Total 9

If the Dealer has a Three, Four, Five or Six showing, double down. If the Dealer has a Two or a Seven or higher showing, take a hit. If you have three or more cards that total 9, with no Aces, hit.

A 9 is a good hand - not a great one, and if the Dealer has the makings of a bad hand (a Three through Six showing), you want to exploit that opportunity by getting more money out in your circle by doubling down.

You Have Two Cards That Total 10

If the Dealer's card is a Nine or less, double down. Joyfully. If the Dealer has a 10-card or an Ace showing, take a hit. If you get three or more cards that total to 10, take a hit.

Your Two-Card Hand Totals 11

Double down on all cards except the Ace. If you have three or more cards that total to 11, you can't double down so take a hit.

[The following strategy chart shows the proper play when the Player's hand has three or more cards making up the total. In these cases, the Player cannot split pairs or double down (or surrender) so the only options available are to hit or stand. Notice that the Player always takes a hit with a 9, 10 and 11.]

Optimum Basic Strategy for Multiple Deck Blackjack
After Player Has Taken A Hit
(No Opportunity to Split or Double Down)

YOUR HAND	DEALER'S UPCARD									
	2	3	4	5	6	7	8	9	10	A
A3	H	H	H	H	H	H	H	H	H	H
A4	H	H	H	H	H	H	H	H	H	H
A5	H	H	H	H	H	H	H	H	H	H
A6	H	H	H	H	H	H	H	H	H	H
A7	S	S	S	S	S	S	S	H	H	H
A8	S	S	S	S	S	S	S	S	S	S
A9	S	S	S	S	S	S	S	S	S	S
A10	S	S	S	S	S	S	S	S	S	S
Below 12	H	H	H	H	H	H	H	H	H	H
12	H	H	S	S	S	H	H	H	H	H
13-16	S	S	S	S	S	H	H	H	H	H
Above 16	S	S	S	S	S	S	S	S	S	S

S = Stand   **H** = Hit

Your Two-Card Hand Totals 12

The first of the special cases. If you take a hit with a 12, the odds are 4 out of 13 that you will get a 10-card and bust. So you want to take a hit when it improves your overall chances of winning. Look at the Chart and notice the division between the Six and the Seven for the Dealer's hand.

Now find the rows where the Player's hand totals 12 and 13 - 16. These are the **stiff hands**. Generally if the Dealer has to take a card, you do not want to hit and chance busting. If the Dealer's upcard is a Seven or higher, he has the potential for a pat hand and you need to take a hit.

But the 12 is special. Since there are only four cards out of thirteen that would bust you, you should take a card if the Dealer has a Two or a Three showing. A Two or a Three for the Dealer is not such a bad hand; it is likely that he will make a hand between 17 and 21 so you want to take one shot at making a hand yourself.

Take a card if you have 12 and the Dealer has a Two or a Three. Stand if the Dealer has a Four, Five or Six. Hit if the Dealer has a Seven or more.

One word of warning: As I mentioned before, only at Blackjack will other players try to tell you how to play your cards and your money. This is one instance where someone is sure to give you a hard time because he is not aware of the optimum strategy.

You Have Two Cards That Total a Hard 13-16

These hands are all played the same way. If the Dealer's card is a Two through Six, stand. If he has an Ace or a Seven or more, take a hit. If you still don't have at least 17, take another hit. Keep taking hits until your cards total 17 or more.

Sometimes it is oh-so-difficult. You've got an Eight-Four and the dealer has a Nine. You take a hit. A Two. You've got 14. Another hit: another two. Now you've got 16. You are absolutely sure that the next card out of the shoe is going to be a 10-card. Maybe so. But remember that in a 6-deck shoe there are 120 cards that are Ace through Five.

Just because two low cards in a row have come out of the shoe does not mean that the next one won't be a low card also. Take a hit. If you don't, you may win this particular hand, but you will lose in the long run.

All of the moves in the Basic Strategy represent the smartest move you can make in each situation over the long haul. There is no way to predict if the Basic Strategy will work out for you on any single hand, but over time the Strategy maximizes your odds of ending up a winner.

You Have Hard 17-21

The chart does not show the cases when you have a hard 17 through 21. These are the 'no brainers'. Stand and hope for the best. Hope, because a 17 or an 18 are not very good hands.

In fact, if you got dealt an 18 every single hand, you would lose in the long run. You have a decent hand, and unless it is a pair of Nines, you are going to sit and wait while the Dealer does his thing.

Hard Hand Strategy Review

Let's do a quick review of the hard hands (assume no pairs):

• If you have a 9, double down if the Dealer has Three through Six, otherwise hit.

• If you have a 10, double down except against a 10-card or an Ace, in which case hit.

• If you have an 11, double down except against the Ace.

• You have 12. If the Dealer has a Four, Five or Six, stand; otherwise hit.

• You have a 13 through 16. Stand if the Dealer has a Six or less. Hit if he has a Seven or more. (An Ace is 'more'.)

• You have a 17 through 21. Stand.

These situations cover almost 92% of the hands that you will get during any Blackjack session. If you know how to play these hands correctly and are familiar with the general rules we covered earlier, you will be among the top few percent of the players. It really is not that hard. It requires a little practice and a lot of faith.

If you start second-guessing the strategy and changing your play because you feel what the next card is going to be, you are in trouble. It is a slippery slope because of the phenomenon known as *selective memory*. You will tend to remember the times when making the wrong play worked and forget the times that it didn't.

The cards do not know that you have a 12 and that 'you always bust when you hit 12's'. The cards do not even know that the last eight cards out of the shoe were all low cards. Trust the mathematics of the game. Learn the strategy, play the strategy, and give yourself a chance to walk away a winner.

Playing the Soft Hands

The next section of the chart covers the *soft* hands, those that contain an Ace. The correct play for some of these situations is not always obvious.

Basically, you'll stand with your good hands and hit the poor ones. To really take advantage of those occasions where the Dealer has problems, you double down aggressively because you get two chances to win - you might get a card that makes your hand valuable in its own right or the Dealer might bust.

Because you have the opportunity to count the Ace as 11 or as 1, the soft hands are more powerful than another hand that has the same total. For instance, an Ace-Four can be counted as 5 or 15, and it is a better hand for the Player than either a 5 or a 15.

You will probably need to study these next few cases more than you do the ones that we have already covered:

You Have an Ace-Two (3 or 13) or Ace-Three (4 or 14)

You always want to take a card, and if the Dealer has a Five or a Six showing, you should double down.

If you are not doubling down and your hit card is a Nine or a 10-card, then you have a hard 12 or 13 and should proceed as described earlier. If you draw any other card, you still have a soft hand and should either hit or stand as shown on the table on Page 69. Remember, you no longer have the option to double down after you have taken a hit.

Ace-Four (5 or 15) or Ace-Five (6 or 16)

You double down if the Dealer has a Four, Five or Six showing. Against any other card you just take a hit.

Your Hand is an Ace-Six (7 or 17)

This is where things start to get interesting. It could be argued that the Player should stand with a 17. After all, the Dealer has to stand if he gets an Ace-Six, so it must make some sense. And, goes the argument, if I take a hit, it might be a Nine, then I've got 16, and I'm really in a hole. Far better to keep the known 17 than go risking this bird in the hand.

Wrong. I've already warned you that a 17 is not a very good hand. If you play Blackjack for long, you will come to dislike hard 17's. You can't take a hit, and yet you are very likely to lose. Treat this hand as a 7: always take a hit.

But treat it as a 7 with potential, and if the Dealer has a Three, Four, Five or Six, double down on the hand. You will probably get a 10-card and you will still have your 17. If you get an Eight or a Nine, you hope for the Dealer to bust. And, once in a while, the fates will smile and you will receive a Two or a Three, and all of a sudden you've taken an ordinary 17 and turned it into a solid 19 or 20.

You should never stand on Ace-Six.

Your Hand is an Ace-Seven (8 or 18)

You have one of the most complicated hands to play in the whole game. The situation is even worse because many Dealers will incorrectly assume that they know what you want to do, and you may have to make your hand signals very clearly and emphatically to make yourself understood.

If the Dealer has a Two, you stand with your 18.

If the Dealer has a Three through Six, you double down (and love it because you are probably going to win).

If the Dealer has a Seven or an Eight, you stand. The theory is that you will beat the Dealer's likely 17 and push his 18, so don't press your luck.

If the Dealer has a Nine, 10-card, or Ace, take a hit. This is a play that may get you in trouble with your fellow Players and some Dealers. They do not understand why you are risking a perfectly good 18.

The reason is quite simple: your good 18 is probably going to lose to a better 19 or 20. Take a hit. If you get a 10-card or a small card, you are no worse off that you started. If you get a middle card (say a Five, so your total is 13), treat it as a hard 13 and play accordingly by continuing to hit until you get to 17 or bust.

The first time you get an Ace-Seven against a Nine, the Dealer is not likely to expect you to take a hit. Make your hand signal firmly as if you know what you are doing, because you do.

You Have Ace-Eight or Ace-Nine (9-19, 10-20)
Stand. These are very good hands, and you don't want to consider them as anything other than a 19 or a 20, respectively.

You Have Ace-10 (21)
If you have Ace-10, you have the ultimate, a Blackjack.

SPLITTING PAIRS
Now let's look at the really fun hands - the pairs. Splitting pairs provides you with the greatest opportunity to get your money out in the circle after you see how good your cards are and how bad the Dealer's are. If the cards fall correctly, you could split up to three times, making four hands, and you could double down on each of them, in effect betting up to eight times your original bet.

I have never quite had it this good, but I have had four hands with two double downs, a total of six bets out on one hand.

Mostly the pairs are easy and are intuitive:

2s, 3s and 7s
If you have a pair of Twos, Threes or Sevens, split if the Dealer's card is Two through Seven, otherwise just take a hit. You split against the Two through Six because the Dealer is going to have to take at least one hit, so the chances are high that he will bust.

The reason for splitting against the Seven is that it is likely that the Dealer will have 17. Your odds of getting at least one hand better than 17 starting with a Two, Three or Seven are excellent and you may get a second card on one of your hands that allows you to double down against the Dealer's Seven.

Once you have received a second card on a split hand, you should play it as if it were the hand originally dealt to you. You finish play on the first of your hands - until you either stand or bust - before you start play on the second hand.

44s

If you have Fours, split them against a Five or a Six, otherwise just take a hit. Two Fours total 8 which is a decent start to a hand. You don't want to break that up in your eagerness to split pairs. On the other hand, if the Dealer's card is bad enough - a Five or Six, the stronger move is to split the Fours and play two separate hands.

55s

If you have Fives, always treat them as a 10. Double down unless the Dealer has as 10-card or Ace showing, in these cases take a hit. Never split Fives.

66s

Split Sixes against the weak dealer upcards Two through Six, but play them as a 12 against the dealer's Seven through Ace. You don't want to start out with two weak totals of Six each against cards the dealer is likely to make hands with.

88s

A pair of Eights is covered by one of the general rules: always split a pair of Eights.

99s

A pair of Nines is another interesting hand. There are those who would say that for a hand to play, there is nothing they'd rather have than a pair of Nines.

If the Dealer has a stiff card - Two through Six, split the pair of Nines. If the Dealer has a Seven or an Eight, stand. Play your Nines as an 18 against the probable 17 or 18.

If the Dealer has a Nine, split your Nines. Your 18 is likely to lose anyhow, and you may get an Ace (for a 20) or a Two (for an 11, so you can double down), and you are likely to get a 10-card to make 19 and push. Split those Nines against a Nine. And expect some reaction from the crowd.

If the Dealer has a 10-card or an Ace, stand. You are likely to lose, and there is no point in making two hands that are likely to lose.

10s

Never split a pair of 10-cards.

Aces

Always split Aces. Another general rule. Remember that when you split Aces, you only get only one card on each hand and cannot double down or take a hit. At least one of the riverboats allows you to split again if you get an Ace on an Ace.

VARIATIONS

The Basic Strategy you have just been reviewing is designed for the most common set of rules that you are likely to encounter on the riverboats or in the casinos of Atlantic City and Nevada.

You will find variations in the rules, however, and it is up to you, the Player, to understand all of the rules in effect at the table at which you are preparing to play. Some of the modifications you may encounter are trivial; some are significant. Let's look at them:

Decks of Cards

Most of the riverboats use six decks shuffled together in the shoe, but you may find double-deck Blackjack, and, on at least two boats, eight decks. The main reason casinos use more decks is to speed up the game because shuffling happens less often.

Use the Basic Strategy you are learning here for any game that has two or more decks.

Double Payoff for 3 Sevens or 6, 7, 8 of the Same Suit

This variation comes and goes on some of the Iowa boats. Stick with the Basic Strategy: if you should to split a pair of Sevens, do so; do not just take a hit trying for the third Seven. The increased potential winnings do not cover the additional risk.

Surrender

As promised, I want to touch on the optimum strategy to use when playing multiple deck Blackjack and you are allowed to Surrender. You will remember that when you Surrender you forfeit one-half of your bet and do not play the hand, and you cannot Surrender if the dealer has a Blackjack.

The guidelines for Surrender are easy:

• If the Dealer has an Ace showing, Surrender any hand totaling 16, except a pair of Eights, which you should split.

• If the Dealer has a 10-card, Surrender all 15's and 16's, except a pair of Eights, which you should split.

• If the Dealer has a Nine, Surrender all 16's, except a pair of Eights, which you should split.

You should play all other hands in accordance with the strategies shown earlier.

Over/Under 13

At some Blackjack tables on some of the boats, the casino offers the opportunity for a side bet known as Over/Under 13. If this option is available, there will be two smaller circles near each of the Player's circles, one marked **Over 13** and one marked **Under 13**.

Before any cards are dealt, a Player can place a bet in either of the smaller circles.

The outcome of an Over/Under 13 bet is determined by the total of the Player's first two cards (counting Aces as 1). The payoff on these bets is one to one. Any Over/Under 13 bet loses if the Player's total is exactly 13.

Of the 169 possible combinations of two cards, 76 of them have a total less than 13, 79 total to over 13, and 14 of them total to 13 exactly. If you bet on Under 13, you are giving the House almost a 10% edge. A bet on Over 13 is at a 6.5% disadvantage. These are bad bets. Avoid the temptation to slip a dollar or two out there just for a change.

If you are a dedicated card counter, there may be times when the count varies enough for a wager on Over or Under 13 to make some sense, especially if the count is very 'bad'.

Dealer Has to Hit a Soft 17

About half of the boats have this rule. If the Dealer has a total of 17 that includes an Ace counted as 11 (for example, Ace, Three, Three), he must continue to hit the hand until he has a hard 17 or more. The House gains .20%, by using this rule.

Be aware of this variation when you sit at a table (it will be written right on the felt of the tabletop), but do not change your style of play because of it.

You Cannot Double Down After Splitting a Pair

Be sure to ask about this rule before you start to play Blackjack. Right now, three boats restrict you from doubling down after a split, but the rules can change, so ask. This variation definitely changes your playing strategy.

You will remember that the Basic Strategy called for you to split lots of pairs against the Dealer's small cards. This makes sense because the Dealer is likely to bust and you might get to double down on one or both of the hands and really go to town.

If you can't double down, some of the allure in splitting is removed. The table on the following page shows the changes to the Basic Strategy if you can't double down after a split:

• Don't split Twos and Threes against the Dealer's Two and Three.

• Don't split Fours.

• Don't split Sixes against the Dealer's Two.

And don't panic. These situations come up rarely. The shift in the odds is small. Let's say you are playing where you cannot double down after splitting a pair and you get a small pair against the Dealer's small card.

If you know what to do: great. If you don't remember, base your decision on your comfort level with the bet that you have out there. The tiny increase in percentages if you make the correct play would be offset by the anxiety you feel worrying about it. Do what feels right;

hope that it doesn't happen again this cruise; and when you get home, pull out this book and brush up on the Optimum Basic Strategy for the next riverboat you are likely to visit.

Optimum Basic Strategy for Multiple Deck Blackjack
Initial Two Card Total
<u>No</u> Double Down After Split Allowed

YOUR HAND	DEALER'S			UPCARD						
	2	3	4	5	6	7	8	9	10	A
AA	spl	spl	spl	spl	spl	spl	spl	spl	spl	spl
22	H	H	spl	spl	spl	spl	H	H	H	H
33	H	H	spl	spl	spl	spl	H	H	H	H
44	H	H	H	H	H	H	H	H	H	H
55	D	D	D	D	D	D	D	D	H	H
66	H	spl	spl	spl	spl	H	H	H	H	H
77	spl	spl	spl	spl	spl	spl	H	H	H	H
88	spl	spl	spl	spl	spl	spl	spl	spl	spl	spl
99	spl	spl	spl	spl	spl	S	spl	spl	S	S
10-10	S	S	S	S	S	S	S	S	S	S

H = Hit   **S** = Stand   **D** = Double   **spl** = Split
Do not split 4-4, 5-5 and 10-10. Always split A-A and 8-8.

In conclusion, I would like to add a personal endorsement for Blackjack. If you are willing to practice the Basic Strategy and use it when you are at the table, you will find an unmatched combination of decent odds, non-stop action, and social interaction.

Plus you have a hand in determining your fate: you can take the next card or you can stand. In the other games on the boats, your win or loss is determined entirely by what shows on the dice, where the ball lands, or which symbols are on the reels.

Always remember the rules of good money management, learn

the Basic Strategy presented here, and get ready to become a winner at the Blackjack tables.

WINNING AT CRAPS

In any casino, you can follow the noise to the Craps tables. There is something about this exciting, fast-paced dice game that makes instant friends of the most casual strangers and has supposedly mature men and women calling out things like *Gimme an eighter from Decatur* or *Hard way, Baby. Mamma wants a 55.*

The Craps table is a large rectangle with the actual playing surface, the **layout**, about a foot or so lower than the railing that surrounds it.

A crew of four casino employees runs the game: the **Stickman**, who controls the dice; two **Dealers**, who pay off winning bets and collect losing ones; and the **Floorman**, who is in charge of the table and settles disputes while keeping a watchful eye on the whole game.

There might be anywhere from one to fifteen players at an active Craps game, and there always seems to be room for one more. Between the Dealers is a supply of chips, and somewhere on the table will be a small sign indicating the minimum bet that can be placed.

While the game of Craps itself is quite simple, the playing surface can be bewildering to the novice. There are anywhere from 36 to 40 areas on the table where you can place wagers. But, as opposed to Blackjack, you don't need to learn a complicated strategy in order to be an expert Craps player. Rather, you need to be aware of which of the 40 possible bets to avoid and where to risk your money.

Take a quick look at the representation of a Craps layout on the following page. You'll notice that the left third of the layout is almost identical to the right third. This provides every Player easy access to the available betting opportunities. A bet on the Pass Line on the right side is the same as a Pass Line bet on the left side.

The middle third of the Craps table is cluttered with a dozen little boxes, pictures of dice and other miscellany. It is not as accessible to the average Player, and that is good. You should not be placing bets in the middle third of the table

The Craps Layout

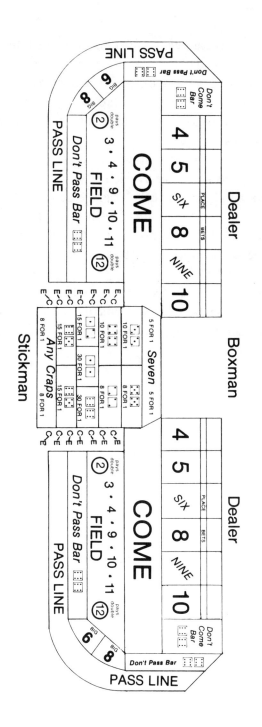

All bets in Craps are won or lost based on the total of the two numbers showing on the top sides of a pair of dice that one of the Players has thrown. Each of the dice is exactly like the dice that you have in board games at home - there are six sides numbered from 1 to 6. The total of the two numbers can be anywhere between 2 (1 and 1) and 12 (two 6's).

We will look at the odds of each of these numbers when we examine which bets should be avoided.

To start the game, one Player is designated as the **Shooter,** the one who will actually throw the dice. After all bets are placed, the Shooter takes the two dice in hand and throws them the length of the table. On your turn, give the dice a good toss; try to bounce them off the far side of the table.

On the first throw, if the Shooter makes a 7 or 11, it is a **natural**, a win for all players who are betting with the Shooter. If the Shooter gets a 2, 3, or 12, he has **crapped out**, and the players betting with the Shooter lose.

If the Shooter's first roll is a 4, 5, 6, 8, 9 or 10, that number becomes the **point**. In this case, he will keep rolling the dice until he makes that number again or gets a 7, whichever comes first.

Betting With the Shooter

To bet with the Shooter, you place a bet on the Pass Line before the Shooter has made the first roll of his turn, called the **come-out roll**. A Pass Line bet is won when the Shooter either rolls a 7 or an 11 on the first roll, a natural, or rolls his point again before he gets a 7 or 11.

If the Shooter's first roll is a 2, 3 or 12, all Pass Line bets lose. Also, once the Shooter has established a point, the roll of a 7, called **sevening out**, is a loser for the Pass Line bet.

Winning Pass Line bets are paid 1 to 1, that is, a winning bet of $10 gets paid $10.

A couple of examples:

Example 1. The Shooter rolls a 3 and a 6 for a total of 9 on his first roll. The point is 9. In order for Pass Line bets to win, he must roll another 9 before he rolls a 7. Any other numbers thrown are irrelevant to Pass Line bets. He may roll the dice 50 times or more until either he rolls a 7 (and Pass Lines bets lose) or a 9 (and Pass Line bets win).

Example 2. The Shooter rolls a 2 and a 5 for a total of 7 on his first roll. 7 is a winner for the Pass Line bets. If you had placed $5 on the Pass Line, a Dealer would put another $5 chip next to your wager and both chips are yours.

At the end of each turn, (after an opening 7 or 11, an opening craps, the Shooter making his point, or the Shooter rolling a 7 instead of his point), there will be a new come-out roll, and new pass line bets may be placed.

On any bet on the Pass Line, the odds favor the House by 1.4%. While this is not a large advantage compared, for instance, to the 5.26% edge the House has in Roulette, it can be reduced even further if the Player betting the Pass Line takes **Odds**, places a supplemental bet after the Shooter establishes a point.

Odds Bets

To maximize your chances of winning, you should make an **Odds bet** before the Shooter makes his second roll. This is done by placing an amount equal to the pass line bet directly behind your original wager near the Pass Line.

If your bets are $10 and the Shooter rolls a 7 before a 9, you will lose both bets, a total of $20. However, if the Shooter makes his point, you will win $10 for your Pass Line bet and $15 on your Odds bet, a total of $25.

Odds bets are so-named because they offer the Player even odds with no advantage to the House. An Odds bet will be paid off at 6 to 5 if the point is six or eight, 3 to 2 if the point is five or nine (as in our example), and 2 to 1 if the point is four or ten.

If you place Pass Line bets, always follow them up with Odds bets when the Shooter establishes a point. This strategy cuts the House advantage to about .8% on every wager.

In Nevada and Atlantic City, you'll find casinos that offer Double or Triple Odds, even up to Ten or Twenty times Odds.

Only Single Odds are offered on the riverboats at this time.

However, if you are shooting Craps where these increased Odds are available, you should always take the maximum amount that is offered by the casino *and* is consistent with the rules of good money management.

Let's take a look at some of the probabilities of the Craps game. There are two dice, each numbered 1 to 6. On any roll, one of the six sides must come up on the first die and one of the six on the second, with a total of 36 possible combinations that can result.

The lowest total is 2, and there is only one of the 36 combinations that gives a total of 2, when each of the dice has a 1 showing.

There are two ways out of the 36 to get a total of 3: there can be a 1 on the first die and a 2 on the second or a 2 on the first die and a 1 on the second.

You will see there are three combinations that result in a total of 4 (3 + 1, 2 + 2, and 1 + 3).

In summary, the possible results are:

Dice Combinations Chart	
Result	**Odds of Result**
2	1 out of 36
3	2 out of 36
4	3 out of 36
5	4 out of 36
6	5 out of 36
7	6 out of 36
8	5 out of 36
9	4 out of 36
10	3 out of 36
11	2 out of 36
12	1 out of 36
Total	**36 out of 36**

Again looking at our earlier example, once the Shooter has established 9 as his point, on each succeeding roll, there are six chances out of 36 that he will get a 7 and only four chances out of 36 that he will get a 9.

Thus, a 7 is 1.5 times more likely to appear than a 9, and a payoff of 3 to 2 on an Odds bet is exactly an even bet with no advantage to anyone. The House still retains its slight edge on the Pass Line bet..

The Pass Line is the easiest and most common way to bet with the Shooter, and when you take Odds, you are making one of the best percentage bets that the casino offers at any of the games.

You may not place an Odds bet without having a Pass Line bet in play.

The other method of betting with the Shooter involves the Come bets which are exactly like the Pass Line bets except that they are made anytime AFTER the Shooter has established a point. A come bet is made by placing the wager in the area marked **come**.

The Come bet wins immediately if the next roll is a 7 or 11 and loses if the next roll is 2, 3 or 12. If any other number comes up, that becomes your **Come Point** and you win if the Shooter rolls your Come Point before he rolls a 7. You may place a series of Come bets and end up with several Come Points during a turn.

The percentages on Come bets are identical with the odds we discussed for the Pass Line bets - a 1.4% house edge.

In addition, you may make an Odds bet exactly like the one available for the Pass Line bet. To take Odds on a Come bet, give your chips to the Dealer with the instruction *Odds, on the Come*. He will place your chips on top of your Come bet but offset so that it can be distinguished from it.

When you make Come bets followed with Odds bets, you are only giving the House a .8% advantage against you.

Betting Against the Shooter

The Craps table offers Don't Pass and Don't Come bets for those who want to bet against the Shooter, the so-called **wrong way** bettors.

These bets operate almost exactly opposite of the Pass and Come bets. You lose if the next roll is a 7 or 11 or the point is rolled before the 7, and win with a 2 or 3 on the first roll or if a 7 comes up before the point is rolled.

The exception is that if the first roll is a 12, it is a tie on the Don't Pass and Don't Come bets and you neither win nor lose. (In some casinos, the 2 is a tie and the 12 a loser.) Remember that a Pass Line bet or a Come bet loses if the first roll of the progression is a 12.

To make a Don't Pass bet, place your chips in the Don't Pass area before any come-out roll. When a point is established, you take Odds by placing chips in the Don't Pass box next to your first bet.

A Don't Come bet is made after the come-out roll by placing your chips in the Don't Come box near either end of the Craps table. When a Don't Come point is established, the Dealer will move your bet to the Don't Come area for that point, and you should take odds by giving your chips to the Dealer and saying something like *Odds on the Don't Come*.

Odds Bets - Wrong Bettors

You should always take Odds on your Don't Pass and Don't Come bets. In fact the House advantage is almost exactly the same with these bets with full Odds as it is with the Pass and Come bets - .8%.

The allowable Odds bet on the Don't Pass and Don't Come wagers are determined by the *payoff*, not the original bet. The payoffs are exactly opposite the Pass and Come bets: 1-2 on 4 and 10, 2-3 on 5 and 9, and 5-6 on 6 and 8.

Thus, to make an Odds wager behind a $5 bet, $10 could be wagered if the point were 4 or 10, $7.50 if the point were 5 or 9, and $6 if the point were 6 or 8.

My preference is to avoid 'Don't' bets and place my wagers with the Shooter. Most players bet with the Shooter and there is a certain amount of camaraderie among these bettors. If a Shooter has a good run of rolls, the noise level and winnings will increase exponentially as players win bet after bet.

Conversely, if Shooters are crapping out regularly and players are losing, there is a tendency to place some blame on someone who happens to be betting against the Shooter and winning while others are losing.

From an odds standpoint, betting with or against the Shooter are equivalent tactics, and you should bet in a manner that makes you most comfortable.

Place Bets

Once a point is established, the casino will allow you to make **place bets**, select your own point from the **point numbers**: 4, 5, 6, 8, 9 and 10.

You 'place' a bet on the number or numbers you choose, and the bet works like a Come point. If the Shooter rolls your number before he rolls a 7, you win. If a 7 comes up first, all Place bets lose.

The payoffs are 9 to 5 on a four or ten, 7 to 5 on a five or nine, and 7 to 6 on a six or eight. The House edge is 6.67% on the four or ten, 4.00% on the five or nine, and 1.52% on the six and eight.

That 1.52% advantage to the House for Place bets on the six or eight is not a horrible bet, but we will see that if you stick to the optimum betting strategy, you will cut the House odds to almost half of that percentage.

To make a Place bet, give your chips to the Dealer and tell him that you want to *Place the Six* or some such instruction that tells him you want to make a Place bet on a specific number.

Place bets may be made any time, but they are not in effect, they are *off* for the come-out roll unless you specify that your Place bet should be *on* for the come-out. Place bets can also be reduced or removed entirely before any roll.

One more thing to watch out for on Place bets: the payoffs are only made in whole dollar amounts, so if you make Place bets in the wrong multiples, you will not get the full payoff.

For instance, the payoff on a Place bet on the Eight is 7 to 6. If you bet $5, you will only win $5 instead of $5.83. That reduced payoff makes the bet a very poor one. If you Place a bet on the Six or Eight, bet a multiple of $6.

Many Players favor the Place bets, and you will often see gamblers who cover all of the numbers with Place bets. Resist the temptation to join in the action. Save your wagers for the bets that give you the highest odds of winning.

OTHER CRAPS BETS

There are several other bets available on the Craps table. Some are multiple roll bets and some are one roll bets. We will look at them here, but you should be aware of them only as a source of amusement as you watch other people wager their hard-earned money on them.

Do not make these miscellaneous bets; the House has anywhere from a 5% to a whopping 17% edge on these wagers.

Betting the Field

A Field bet wins if the next roll is a 2, 3, 4, 9, 10, 11 or 12, and loses if the roll is 5, 6, 7 or 8. Of the eleven possible totals, the Field bet wins on seven of them, and if the total is 2 or 12, the Field bet wins double.

What can go wrong? Plenty. The four losing numbers represent 20 of the possible 36 combinations of the dice. Even taking the double payoff for a total of 2 or 12 into account, the House has a 5.55% edge on Field bets. (Sometimes the casino pays triple on the 2 or 12, reducing the house edge to 2.7% - still not such a good bet.)

Hardways

A player can make a Hardway bet on 4, 6, 8 or 10. If the number selected is rolled with a pair, for example, *4 the Hardway*, and a 2 and 2 is rolled, the bet wins. If the number comes up any other way or if a 7 comes up, the bet loses.

Don't bet the Hardways. The payoffs are big (7 to 1 for four and ten, 9 to 1 for six and eight), but you are giving your money to the house. The House odds for the Hardways range from 9.09% to 11.11%.

Proposition Bets

Look again at the Craps layout and you will see miscellaneous bets in the center section called **Proposition bets**. These one-roll bets are bad news.

Any Seven pays 4 to 1, but equitable odds would be 5 to 1 a 16.67% edge for the house. **Any Craps** (2, 3, or 12) pays 7 to 1, but the true odds are 8 to 1, which translates to an 11.1% disadvantage for the Player. And so on down the line.

Save your money, and keep your chips away from the center of the Craps table.

Big 6 and Big 8

Famous sucker bets. You drop a chip or two on the handy little space near the corner of the table, and you win even money if a 6 or 8, whichever you chose, comes up before a 7. If the 7 is first, you lose.

Not only does the house have a 9.09% edge on this bet (there are six ways to make a 7 and only five ways to make a 6) but you can make the SAME bet by making a Place bet on the 6 or 8 and get a better payoff if you win - 7 to 6.

Don't be tempted by the Big 6 and the Big 8.

The Winning Strategy at Craps

As you may have guessed, your best strategy at Craps involves the Pass and Don't Pass Lines and the Come and Don't Come bets. Remember that the House edge is identical for Pass bets and Don't Pass bets, just as the odds are the same for Come and Don't Come bets.

Whether you bet with or against the Shooter is a matter of your comfort level. There is no advantage either way in the long run.

One factor to consider in betting is that you always want to make wagers that will get paid off with the full return due you. Many Craps tables make payoffs in whole dollars only. At these tables, if you make a $5 Odds bet when the point is 9, you will only get paid $7 instead of $7.50 if a 9 is rolled before a 7.

In most of the land-based casinos, you would have the opportunity to raise your Odds bet to $6 in this instance. By making an Odds bet of $6, you can earn the full correct payout - $9, if the 9 is rolled before a 7.

At this time, the riverboat casinos are not this enlightened. You are restricted to Odds bets that are no larger than your original Pass/Don't Pass or Come/Don't Come bets.

The third thing to keep in mind is the guidelines for smart money management. Your basic betting unit should be about one-fortieth of your stake.

This is especially important at Craps. If you make a Pass bet with full Odds and two or more Come bets, also backed by full Odds, you may have as many as eight bets on the table. If your basic bet is too large in relation to your bankroll, you run a high risk of getting wiped out in a short adverse run.

Winning Strategy For Iowa

Let us first consider the riverboats in Iowa. The $5 maximum bet makes the ideal strategy particularly simple. If you are betting with the Shooter, verify that the table has $2.50 chips - they all do - and bet $5 on the Pass Line.

When the point is established follow your Pass bet with a $5 Odds bet and start placing $5 Come bets until you have two or three numbers covered. Take $5 Odds on each number as it becomes your point.

Depending upon the numbers rolled, the payoffs for a $5 bet are $5 (Pass and Come), $6 (Points 6 and 8), $7.50 (5 and 9), or $10 (4 and 10). Because the Iowa riverboats use $2.50 chips, all of these payoffs can be made easily.

Since you are limited to a maximum bet of $5, you do not have to worry about when to increase your bet. When you get up an amount equal to half of your stake, start to put money aside that will not be touched.

If you double your bankroll, you should decide if you want to take a break and quit a sure winner or set aside your original stake, increase your unit bet, and press your luck. Keep setting money aside, and you may hit a streak and leave the riverboat after a truly memorable session.

In any event, do not give back more than your original limit - this insures that you come out ahead.

If you want to bet against the Shooter in Iowa, you should bet $3 on the Don't Pass line and follow it up with full Odds. Then start making Don't Come bets until you have two or three numbers covered.

The payoffs for a $3 bet against the Shooter are $3 (don't pass and don't come), $2.50 (points 6 and 8), $2 (5 and 9) and $1.50 (4 and 10).

If you make $5 wrong way bets, you are increasing the House odds against you because they will not be able to give you the full payout. For instance, if you make a $5 Don't Pass bet and the point is 6, your $5 Odds bet should be paid at 5 to 6 or $4.16, but you will only be paid $4 for your Odds bet.

To recap: In Iowa, if you are betting with the Shooter, make $5 bets and follow them up with $5 Odds bets. If you are betting against the Shooter, bet $3 and make $3 Odds bets. This is because Iowa state law restricts you to a maximum bet of $5.

Winning Strategy for Illinois and Other States

Outside of Iowa, your winning strategy is still going to be based on Pass Line and Come bets if you are betting with the Shooter and on Don't Pass and Don't Come bets if you choose to bet against the Shooter. By always taking advantage of Odds bets and making wagers that offer you full payoffs, you will hold the House percentage against you to a mere .8%.

Let's look at the strategy briefly:

To bet with the Shooter, your Pass Line bet should be a multiple of $10. When a point is established, follow up your Pass bet with an Odds bet of $10. By making bets that are a multiple of $10, you will get the full payoff you are due on your Odds bet no matter what the point happens to be.

After a point is established, you will want to start placing Come bets the same size as your original Pass Line bet. As you establish a Come point, follow it up with full Odds, and place another Come bet until you have two or three Come points established.

As your earnings increase, you can increase the size of your unit bet consistent with good money management, but always keep your bet to a multiple of $10.

If the riverboats use either $.50 or $2.50 chips, you can bet in multiples of $5 and still receive the full payout.

If you want to place wrong way bets (against the Shooter) outside of Iowa, the rule of thumb is that your bets should be multiples of $6. They can be $6 or $600, but if you make Don't Come and Don't Pass bets that are not a multiple of 6, you are forfeiting some of the benefit of the Odds bets.

When a point is established, take full Odds on the Don't Pass bet and start placing Don't Come bets and placing Odds bets on your Don't Come points as they are established. Continue to place Don't Come bets until you have two or three numbers covered, depending upon your level of aggressiveness.

Winning Summary

In any state, on any riverboat, at any Craps table, avoid the rest of the bets the casino so generously offers you. They may look like a sure thing, and, in the casino's eyes, they just about are - you are sure to lose in the long run.

At the Craps table, stick with the Pass and Don't Pass bets and the Come and Don't Come bets. Don't lose more than you budgeted for the cruise, and when you get ahead, start pocketing money that you will not touch. Always play to win.

Craps is popular. It can be exciting, and, when you stick to the advantageous bets, Craps is an easy game to learn. If you find that Blackjack is not your cup of tea, Craps offers you a very different way to gamble with some of the best odds available.

WINNING AT SLOT MACHINES AND VIDEO POKER

Who hasn't heard the story of the little, old lady with white gloves standing in front of a slot machine pulling the handle for hours at a stretch? It happens. There are also big, young men who play the one-armed bandits for an entire cruise. And everyone of every age, size, and sex in between.

The Slot Machines are easy - everything you need to know is written right on the front of them, and no one will pressure you to hurry up. They are fun. And they are addicting.

On every spin there is the possibility that you are going to win the jackpot. Even if you don't, you might hit one of the lesser payouts that reinforce that feeling that the *big one* is just around the corner.

Each riverboat has hundreds of slot machines, in denominations ranging from 25¢ to $5 for a pull of the handle. You will quickly learn though, that the 'size' of the machine is only a guide to how much it actually costs to play the thing.

Often, to earn the maximum payoffs, you must play multiple coins (generally three, sometimes five) every time you pull the handle. Each of the machines falls into one of four basic types:

- Traditional slots
- Progressives
- Video poker
- Other.

TRADITIONAL SLOT MACHINES

The traditional slot machine is a single machine with all of the payoffs clearly represented right on the machine. Most often, increasing the number of coins you play on a spin will increase the jackpot proportionately.

For instance, if a winning combination of three Cherries pays 10 coins when you bet 1 coin, it almost certainly pays 20 coins when you bet 2 coins, etc.

The exception might be for the highest payoff. It is possible that, for instance, three Bars would pay 1000 coins for 1 coin, 2000 coins for 2 coins, and 5000 (not 3000) coins for 3 coins played.

If this is the case, you should always play the maximum number of coins. If the payoffs are strictly in line, if the payoff were 3000 in the example given, there is no advantage in playing multiple coins, and you can feel free to play as many coins as you wish on each spin.

While the pay-offs for a slot machine are clearly shown on the front, the odds of winning are more carefully hidden. The odds of getting any particular combination depend upon the number of reels, the number of symbols on each reel, and the number of the winning symbols on each reel.

If you are playing a mechanical slot machine that has reels that actually spin when you pull the handle, then there is a physical limit to the number of symbols that can be on a reel.

If the slot is a video machine, one where the "reels" are just TV pictures that flash by, there is no size limit to each reel.

Today's slot machines will do everything but take out the laundry. You are certain to find machines that offer multiple pay-out lines. Generally a winning combination, say, three Cherries, will pay off only if it is displayed straight across the center of the reel window.

If a machine has multiple pay-out lines, three Cherries might be a winner if they appeared at the top or bottom of the window or even down a diagonal on some machines. Be prepared, though, to bet multiple coins on each spin in order to activate the multiple pay-out lines.

If you have any doubt, read the front of the machine carefully, and do not hesitate to ask the casino personnel.

Many of the machines also allow you to dispense with two traditional slot machines moves: inserting a coin and pulling a handle. These days, you can find machines that offer you the option of allowing credits to build up in the machine rather than dumping the coins into the pay-out tray.

A typical slot machine will have several winning combinations with assorted payoffs. Because of the multitude of payouts available, slot machines are rated based on the percentage of coins fed into them that are actually paid back to the players.

The slot machines on riverboats in Iowa and Illinois are rated at about 91% - which means that on average $91 is paid out for every $100 that is dropped in the slot. In some of the slot palaces in Las Vegas, you will find machines rated at 97% or even higher.

The best strategy on the traditional slots is to avoid letting that percentage grind away at you. Pick the size slot machine you want to play - let's say you choose a $1 slot. Start with a budget of 50-60 times your basic unit - $50 or $60 in this case.

If the payoffs are exact multiples of the coins that you can play, play one coin each spin. If there is an extra large payoff for playing more coins, then play the maximum number each spin.

Play until your money is gone or until you get up $30 (or 30 times your basic unit). Either way - stop. Take a break for a half hour or so. If you're losing, you'll lose less. If you're ahead, you give the machines less time to earn it all back.

PROGRESSIVE SLOT MACHINES

The progressive slots are similar to the traditional ones except that there is a super jackpot that is tied to several machines and grows as coins are inserted into any of them.

Should you choose to play a progressive machine, the strategy is the same as just outlined except that you must play the maximum number of coins on each spin because the Progressive Jackpot will only be paid if all of the coins are played on that spin.

As you might expect, the odds of winning the Jackpot are quite small, but often the payoff itself is similar to the lottery, and you might find that your whole life is changed because of three coins in the right place at the right time.

VIDEO POKER

Video Poker is a type of slot machine that is different from all the others in almost every way - there are no reels, you do not pull a handle to initiate play, and you do have an impact in determining what happens during the play.

After you drop one or more tokens in the slot, you press the button marked **DEAL** and are dealt a single hand of Five Card Draw Poker. If the maximum amount of coins are inserted, five, the cards will be dealt automatically.

You decide which cards you wish to keep and press the button marked **HOLD** under those cards. Then press the DEAL button and the machine will deal replacements for the cards that you discarded.

The payoff is based upon the value of the best poker hand in your final hand, for instance, a Straight might pay you four coins for each coin you bet.

If you want to keep all five your cards, you need to press all five of the HOLD buttons. If you change your mind or press the wrong button, just press the button again and the card will be released. Once you press the DEAL button, the machine will give you replacements for the cards you didn't keep. The payout is based upon the value of the best poker hand in your final five cards.

Video Poker is extremely popular and is quite easy to enjoy, but you must be familiar with the rules or you are just throwing away your money.

The winning hands in ascending order are:

Winning Video Poker Hands

Pair (generally of Jacks or better) - Two cards of the same value in a hand with 3 other cards of different values (Q Q 3 4 7).

Two Pair - Just like it says, two pairs with a fifth card that does not match either of them (8 8 3 3 J).

Three of a Kind - Three cards of the same value and two others of different values (K K K 10 2).

Straight - All five cards with consecutive values regardless of suits. An Ace can be either Low (A 2 3 4 5) or High (10 J Q K A), but the straight cannot loop around (for instance K A 2 3 4 is NOT a Straight).

Flush - All five cards in the same suit, but not a Straight (4 5 9 J K, all of Diamonds).

Full House - A hand with Three of a Kind and a Pair (K K K Q Q).

Four of a Kind - Four cards of the same value and any fifth card (10 10 10 10 9).

Straight Flush - A Straight with all of the cards in the same suit (4 5 6 7 8 all of spades).

Royal Flush - A Straight Flush that runs from the 10 to the Ace (10 J Q K A, all of Hearts).

The object in Video Poker is to get a hand of the highest type. Period. It doesn't matter if you have a pair of 3's and a pair of 2's, it is still Two Pair and the payoff is exactly the same as if you had a pair of Aces and a pair of Kings.

There is no element of bluffing in Video Poker. You should keep only those cards that directly increase your chances of getting a better type of hand.

Here is a typical payout you can expect to find on a Video Poker game on the riverboats today.

Typical Payout for Jacks or Better	
(for each coin bet)	
Pair of Jacks or better	1 coin
Two Pair	2 coins
Three of a Kind	3 coins
Straight	4 coins
Flush	5 coins
Full House	8 coins
Four of a Kind	25 coins
Straight Flush	50 coins
Royal Flush	250 coins

You may find machines with payouts that are higher than these. If so, you will always want to play at the machine that offers the highest payouts available.

The other important thing to remember is that your payout is based on the numbers shown on the machine, not on any bets that you can encourage other players to make. Therefore your play should be based upon the odds of improving your hand compared to the payouts for your machine.

The guidelines presented here are very different than those you may use during a friendly poker game in your basement, because while the ultimate objective - to be a winner - is the same, the games are quite different.

First, note the payout schedule shown on the Video Poker machine. All of the payouts will be exact multiples of the number of tokens played with the exception of the payout for a Royal Flush. In this case, the payoff takes a dramatic jump between the fourth and the fifth token played.

For instance, a Royal Flush with four tokens played pays 1000 tokens while the same hand with five tokens played might have a payoff of 4000 tokens.

If the payout jumps for the fifth coin and you are serious about winning at Video Poker, you should always play five tokens per hand. If your Video Poker machine is a progressive one, with a jackpot that grows as each hand is played, the fifth token payoff for a Royal Flush could be even greater.

At this time there are no progressive Video Poker machines on the riverboats, but that may change tomorrow, and you will find them in other casinos. At a progressive Video Poker machine, you must play all five coins to maximize your odds.

Video Poker Strategy Guidelines

Following are the basic strategy guidelines for the Video Poker machines you will find on the riverboats:

1. If you have four cards to a Royal Flush and you don't have a Straight Flush, discard the fifth card even if it gives you a Straight, a Flush or a high Pair and try for the Royal Flush.

2. If your hand is already a winner and doesn't have four to a Royal Flush, do not break up the winning portion of the hand. For instance, do not break up a Full House to try for Four of a Kind.

3. If you are drawing to a Pair or Three of a Kind, do not keep an outside high card.

4. If you have three cards to a Royal Flush, discard all Pairs and go for the Royal.

5. If you have two cards to a Royal Flush, keep four straights, four flushes, or any winning hand. Otherwise, try for the Royal Flush.

6. If you have a four flush or four straight with a Pair of Jacks or better, keep the Pair. Keep a low Pair over a four straight, but break up the low Pair in favor of a four flush.

7. If you have five odd cards, keep (in declining order of preference) four flush, four straight, two to a Royal Flush, two cards jack or higher, one card Jack or higher, and discard the rest.

If your hand has none of these combinations, discard all five cards and draw new ones.

OTHER SLOT MACHINES

There are also Slot Machines that are video versions of some of the other casino games.

Video Blackjack

Video Blackjack is a popular way to get the feel of a Blackjack game without the pressure of having to make quick decisions.

You can hit, stand, split, and double down just like in a real game. Be sure to check the payout for Blackjack, though. If your machine pays 3 to 2, you should always bet an even number of tokens to insure that you get the correct payout.

Prospective card counters should be aware that every hand on a Video Blackjack machine is dealt from a newly shuffled deck; there is no point in practicing your counting skills on them.

Video Keno

Some of the riverboats offer Video Keno machines. Keno is similar to the Lotto game found in several states: you select a group of numbers in the range one to eighty; the machine then selects twenty of the eighty numbers at random, and your payoff is determined by how many numbers were picked.

The odds on this game are terrible for the Player - generally the House has about a 20% advantage.

If you find yourself tempted by Video Keno, get an ample supply of Slot Machine tokens, wander up to the Hurricane Deck and find a comfortable place along the railing. Every few seconds throw a token into the river. You will earn about the same return as you do at Video Keno, and will be getting some fresh air at the same time.

Slots and Video Poker - Summary

The general rule is to check if the payoff jumps when the 'last' coin, the third or fifth, is played. If so, to maximize your chances of winning, you should play the maximum number of coins every pull.

If the payoffs increase directly in line with the number of coins that you play, feel free to play as many coins as you wish on each turn.

Remember that the House has the advantage at the Slots. If you should happen to get ahead a measurable amount, whatever that may mean to you, take a break. Watch the scenery for a bit, have something to drink, and then return to the machines if you want.

Do not fall into the trap of playing with their money. Once you have scooped the coins from the tray, it is your money. And it is your choice if you want to give them a chance to get it back.

WINNING AT ROULETTE

Roulette migrated to the United States from Europe, where it continues to be the most popular casino game. The game is easy to understand and it has the advantage of moving relatively slowly, so that if you are cautious, you will lose your money somewhat slowly.

Certainly it is possible to win at Roulette in the short run, but if you play Roulette for very long, you will lose money. There are few games that offer consistently worse odds than the Roulette table.

The Roulette table has a large playing surface which the Players gather around, with the wheel at one end. The Roulette Dealer stands next to the wheel, and there is often a plastic shield around the end of the table near the wheel so that stray hands cannot influence the course of the ball.

The 'wheel' is really a disk, carefully balanced on ball bearings so that it will spin freely in its large bowl-shaped container.

Around the circumference of the disk are 38 slots, numbered 0, 00, and from 1 to 36. The numbers are mixed around the edge of the wheel: for instance most wheels will have the sequence 4, 16, 33, 21, 6 etc.

Each numbered slot is colored either red or black, 18 of each color, again in a random order - number 8 is black, 9 is red, 10 and 11 are black, 12 is red. The slots for 0 and 00 are green.

Most of the playing surface is three columns of squares, each containing twelve of the numbers from 1 to 36. At the end nearest the wheel are two pentagons that contain 0 and 00, and along one side and the bottom are other rectangles with brief phrases such as 'Odd' or '1st 12'.

The Roulette Layout

		0		00
1 to 18	1st 12	1	2	3
		4	5	6
EVEN		7	8	9
		10	11	12
◇	2nd 12	13	14	15
		16	17	18
◆		19	20	21
		22	23	24
ODD	3rd 12	25	26	27
		28	29	30
		31	32	33
19 to 36		34	35	36
		2-1	2-1	2-1

Near the Dealer are stacks of chips of assorted colors. When a Player wishes to participate, he decides what the value of each chip is going to be, within the limits set by the House, and is assigned a color. All bets by that Player and only bets by that Player will be made with chips of that color.

For instance, one Player might be assigned blue chips each with a value of $1 while another might use brown chips worth 25¢ each.

Any Player can place wagers on individual numbers or on certain groups of numbers or both. Often each Player will place several bets at various points across the whole board. The unique color of chips for each Player allows one to readily keep track of his or her bets.

At some point the Dealer will give the ball a spin around the inside of the dish containing the wheel and then announce that no more bets can be made. The ball will spin and spin and spin and finally fall into one of the 38 slots. The Dealer places a little marker on the number on the playing surface corresponding to the slot containing the ball, rakes in all of the bets that did not win on that spin, and pays off any of the wagers that were more fortunately placed.

Every bet placed either wins or loses on every drop of the ball. After retrieving any winnings, Players may start placing wagers for the next spin of the ball.

The Odds at Roulette

In Roulette, each drop of the ball is completely independent of every other drop of the ball that has ever happened or ever will happen. In fact, the sequence of numbers from an honest, well-balanced wheel is as close to a truly random pattern as you are likely to find in this world.

What this means is that you must never place a larger-than-usual bet because *you are sure that Black is going to come up*. If ten spins in a row are Red, it is an unusual event (1 in 1024 spins), but the odds of the next spin being Black remain EXACTLY the same (16 out of 38 or 47.37%) if the wheel is fair.

You can be certain that the Roulette wheels on riverboats and in legitimate casinos are as even and as honest as they can humanly be designed.

Since there are thirty-eight slots on the wheel, if the wheel is completely fair, the odds of any given number coming up are 1 in 38. Any discrepancy or structural flaw that would bias the wheel would make some number or numbers more likely to come up than others. It might take a while, but eventually someone would notice that a number was disproportionately represented and start to capitalize on that fact.

The casinos want the wheel to be as fair as possible, because they make a tidy profit on the difference between the fact that the odds against a given number coming up are 37 to 1, yet the payoffs for all of the Roulette bets are at odds of the equivalent of 35 to 1.

That is, if you placed $1 on a number for 38 spins, you would expect to win exactly one time. You would be paid $35, but you would have lost $37 on the other spins that did not go your way. That difference is a 5.26% edge for the House, and that is why Roulette is such a hard game at which to win.

Because at the 0 and 00, the house enjoys the same 5.26% edge on all roulette bets with the exception of the 5 number bet, which is even worse, 7.89%.

Let's go through the various types of bets Players can make.

Single Numbers

A bet is placed directly in the square containing that number. (Bets may be placed on 0 and 00 just as on any other number.)

Be careful that your chip does not touch the lines between the squares because that means something entirely different. The payoff is 35 to 1 (you win thirty-five chips of your color and keep the one you bet).

Two Numbers (Split Bet)

If you place your bet directly on the line that separates two numbers, you are betting on both of them. For instance, you can place one or more chips on the horizontal line separating the 5 and the 6 or on the vertical line dividing the 00 from the 3, and you are betting that either of those numbers will come up. The payoff is 17 to 1.

Three Numbers

By placing your bet on the line at either end of a row of three numbers (for instance 28, 29, and 30), you are betting on all three of them with a payoff of 11 to 1 should one of them come up.

Four Numbers

To bet on a group of four numbers, place your wager directly on the intersection of the two lines that separate the four numbers. For instance, if you put a chip on the cross formed by the lines separating the 8, 9, 11 and 12, you are betting that one of the four will come up for a payoff of 8 to 1.

Five Numbers

Many Players are not even aware of this bet, and since the odds on it favor the House by 7.89%, you should promptly forget that you read about it here.

If you place a bet on the line separating the 0 and 00 from 1, 2 and 3 at either end of the row, you are betting on 0, 00, 1, 2 and 3. The payoff is a paltry 6 to 1.

Six Numbers (Block Bet)

A bet placed on the line separating two rows of numbers and at either end of the row is a bet on all 6 of the numbers involved. The payoff is 5 to 1.

Twelve Numbers

There are two ways to bet on groups of twelve numbers: the **Dozens Bet** and the **Column Bet**.

Along the long side of the playing surface, you will see rectangles that say *1st 12*, *2nd 12* and *3rd 12*. A bet placed in one of these is a bet on, respectively, numbers 1-12, 13-24 and 25-36.

Along the end of the playing surface opposite the 0 and 00, you will see smaller boxes marked *2 to 1*. If you place your wager in one of these boxes, you are betting on the twelve numbers in that column.

Notice that the 0 and 00 are not considered to be in any of the three columns. The payoff for each of these types of bets is 2 to 1.

High or Low

By placing a bet in the appropriate box, you are betting that the number will either be **Low**, 1 to 18, or **High**, 19 to 36. (0 and 00 are neither High nor Low). If you guess correctly, you win 1 to 1.

Even or Odd

This is a bet that the next number will be **Even** or **Odd**. As usual, the 0 and 00 are automatic losers, and a winner pays 1 to 1.

Red or Black

Another variation that works about the same way. If you bet on **Black** (or **Red**) and the ball lands in a Black (Red) slot, you win 1 to 1. Note that the 0 and 00 are green; they are neither red nor black.

ROULETTE STRATEGY

Since all of the percentages except for the Five Number bet are the same, there is only one strategy to pursue - and one caution to remember:

When you sit down at the Roulette table, have a definite goal in mind, try to get there as quickly as you can, and, if you succeed, get up and leave.

With a House edge of 5.26%, it does not take long for the percentage to wear you down, but if you do hit a couple of good payoffs early, get up and get away from the table. The game will still be open if you want to come back and try it again later.

No matter what else you do or what else you learn from this book, do not place an unusually large bet because you are sure that 'it has to come up Red (or High or Even)'. It does not have to.

In fact the odds are 47.37% that it will come up Red and almost 52.63% that it won't. And those odds remain the same every single spin!

WINNING AT BACCARAT AND MINI-BACCARAT

Baccarat is another game of European origin, where it's still quite popular. For most Americans, however, the image of Baccarat involves James Bond sitting down at a high stakes game in Monte Carlo.

In the casinos of Las Vegas and Atlantic City, you will find Baccarat areas set off with velvet ropes and forbidding looking Floormen whose presence does not encourage hanging around. The Baccarat Dealers often wear tuxedos, adding to the image of exclusivity, and most visitors to the casinos never give the game a try.

Yet the high tone of the game is strictly for show. Baccarat is an easy game to learn, and once you have placed your bet, there is no strategy involved in the play of a hand; all moves are pre-determined.

The casinos developed a less intimidating version of the game called Mini-Baccarat and it is this version of the game that you will find on some of the riverboats today.

It is played exactly like its namesake, but on a table that looks like a Blackjack table and is usually located in the pit right alongside a Blackjack game. The betting limits are likely to be lower, and the Dealer is dressed like all of the other Dealers in the area.

Regulation Baccarat Table

The Baccarat table is a huge oval with a notch cut out of one of the long sides. There are fourteen playing areas around the outside of the table, numbered from 1 to 15 with no position 13.

Moving in from the edge, there is a section marked **PLAYER** or **PLAYERS** and an area marked **BANKERS**. In the center of the table there are small boxes numbered 1 to 15 (no 13) and an area that reads **Any Tie**. The Dealer's chip rack is opposite the cut-out, and there will be a shoe on the table from which all of the cards are dealt.

Three Dealers work a single Baccarat table. The **Caller** stands in the notch and announces each play that is to be made and the results. The other two Dealers stand by the chip rack to make change, collect losing bets, and pay off winners.

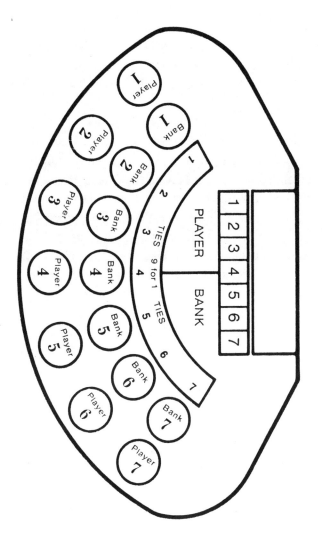

The Mini-Baccarat Layout

Mini-Baccarat Table

The **Mini-Baccarat** table looks like a Blackjack table. It is a semi-circle with six or seven Player's spots around the curved side and the chip rack along the straight side.

At each Player's position there are areas where you can bet on **PLAYER** or **BANKER** or **ANY TIE**. Near the Dealer is a small square for each of the Player's spots, and there is a shoe that holds the cards to be dealt. Only one Dealer will work a Mini-Baccarat game.

The Rules of the Game

In the United States, both Baccarat and Mini-Baccarat are played by the same rules, so I shall drop the term *Mini* from here on out.

In Baccarat, the value of a hand is determined by adding together the two or three cards that make up the hand. The cards Ace through 9 are worth their face value, and Tens, Jacks, Queens and Kings count as 0. A hand is valued only by the final digit of its total.

For example, a hand that has a 7 and a 6 totals 13, so the hand is a 3 (drop the '1'); a hand that has a 3 and a 5 is an 8; a hand that has a 4 and a 6 is a 0 (6 + 4 = 10, but you only look at the digit on the right).

In a round, two hands of two cards each are dealt from the shoe. The first is called the PLAYER's hand, and the second is the BANKER's hand. Before the cards are dealt, each Player places a bet on either the PLAYER or the BANKER. (The hand that is called PLAYER has nothing to do with the Players.)

According to a set of pre-determined rules a third card may be dealt to either or both hands and the totals are compared. The hand with the total closer to 9 wins, and all bets that were placed on the winning hand are paid off at 1 to 1.

The rules give a slight edge to BANKER. Because of this, the House collects a 5% commission on the winning bets if the BANKER hand wins. That is, if a Player bets $10 on BANKER and BANKER wins, he is paid $10 minus 5% (50¢), so the payoff is really $9.50 on a $10 bet.

In reality, the Dealers don't spend all of their time making change to collect the 5%. Instead, they keep a tally in the small squares in the center of the table and each Player is expected to settle up at the end of each shoe or before leaving the table

If the totals are the same, the round is a push and no one wins or loses, unless a tie bet was made.

There is one other betting opportunity available in Baccarat. Players have the opportunity to bet on **Any Tie**. If the BANKER and PLAYER hands end up with the same total, all *Any Tie* bets are paid at 8 to 1.

Rules For Additional Cards

The rules covering when a card is drawn by either hand are summarized on our chart. We will discuss them briefly here, but you do not have to learn them, for the Caller will tell players when an additional card is needed.

If either the PLAYER or BANKER has a two card total of 8 or 9, it is referred to as a **natural** and is an automatic winner unless it ties with or loses to another natural.

Assuming no natural is dealt, the PLAYER stands - does not draw a card - with a total of 6 or 7. Remember the actual total could be 16 or 17, only the last digit counts. If the PLAYER total is 0, 1, 2, 3, 4 or 5, the PLAYER draws a card.

The BANKER always draws with a total of 0, 1 or 2, and draws with a total of 3, 4 or 5 if the PLAYER stands (since the PLAYER must have a 6 or 7). The BANKER stands with a total of 7 and stands with a 6 if the PLAYER did not draw a card.

In the other cases, the BANKER's action depends upon the card that the PLAYER drew. If the BANKER total is 3, BANKER takes a card unless the PLAYER drew an 8. When the BANKER total is 4, BANKER draws unless the PLAYER drew an Ace, 8, 9 or 10-card.

RULES FOR DRAWING A CARD AT BACCARAT

PLAYER RULES

If the Player Has a Total of:	Player Action
0, 1, 2, 3, 4 or 5	Player draws a card
6 or 7	Player stands
8 or 9 (Natural)	Player stands, Banker cannot draw.

BANKER RULES

If the Banker Has a Total of:	Banker Action
0, 1 and 2	Banker draws a card
3	Banker draws when Player stands or when Player's third card is anything except an 8
4	Banker draws when Player stands or when Player's third card is a 2-7
5	Banker draws when Player stands or when Player's third card is a 4-7
6	Banker stands if Player stands and draws if Player's third card is a 6 or 7
7	Banker stands
8 or 9	Banker stands and Player cannot draw

Your Strategy at Baccarat

After deducting the commission, the House has an edge of 1.17% on bets placed on BANKER and an advantage of 1.36% on bets placed on PLAYER. While these odds are not as good as those you will find at Craps or at Blackjack, they are much better than the odds available at the other casino games.

The optimum strategy for Baccarat or Mini-Baccarat is very simple.

• Don't place an 'Any Tie' bet ever (the house has a 14.1% edge).

• Play your hunches but concentrate on BANKER. During the course of a shoe, the hands will tend to even out, but BANKER will win slightly over half, and even with the commission, you have a teeny edge betting on BANKER.

Once again, my usual caution: do not place an extra large bet on BANKER just because BANKER has not won a hand for a while. Each hand is independent of the hands before it.

For those looking for a winning edge by counting cards at baccarat, there is an excellent advanced strategy advertised in the back of the book.

In conclusion, do not be intimidated by the unfamiliar settings of the Baccarat game. Find a table with a betting range with which you are comfortable and enjoy some of the best odds you'll find in the casino. And, by all means, order your martini *shaken, not stirred.*

WINNING AT BIG 6

The Big 6 wheel looks like the 'Wheel of Fortune' from television. A Dealer spins the wheel which stops at one of the 54 spots around the circumference. Each spot indicates the winning number for the spin and also the payoff for any winning bets on that spin.

The name is derived from the fact that there are traditionally 6 possible payoffs.

BIG 6 BETS AND PAYOFFS
- 1 to 1 (24 spots out of the 54)
- 2 to 1 (15 spots)
- 5 to 1 (7 spots)
- 10 to 1 (4 spots)
- 20 to 1 (2 spots)
- 45 or sometimes 40 to 1. There will be two of these, but each is unique and you have to pick the right one to win.

All a Player has to do is place a wager on the area of a table in front of the wheel that corresponds to the payoff that he thinks in likely to come up. The Dealer's job is to spin the wheel, see that no one tries to change his bet as the wheel is slowing, and collect the losing wagers for his employer.

This last event happens quite regularly because the best odds for the Player are 11% in the House's favor.

The optimum strategy for this game is simple: avoid it. It offers the worst odds of any game on the riverboats - except for Video Keno.

WINNING SUMMARY

There are those who say that everything we do in life is a gamble.

Whether or not you believe that, there is an advantage in having a place to gamble where the rules are precisely known, where you decide when and how much to wager, where you decide when to quit, and where the only thing at risk is a little money.

If you keep the financial side of things in perspective and do not risk money that you cannot afford to lose, you can derive a lot of entertainment and excitement from casino gambling.

Most players gamble for the entertainment value of the game rather than the possibility of a life-altering financial gain. At the Roulette table, the ball will fall about thirty times an hour. You can easily pull a Slot Machine's handle 200 times in an hour.

Each fall of the ball, each pull of the handle, each turn of a card offers you the thrill of victory or the bittersweet taste of defeat. That constant rise and fall of emotions provides an adrenalin rush that keeps us coming back to a situation where the odds are often stacked against us.

But, believe me, the entertainment and thrill of gambling is enhanced if you walk away with some of the casino's money. It does not have to be a large amount; you will derive great pleasure from the fact that you took the House on at its own game and you won - even if you just won the amount that you paid for admission to the boat.

The House has designed the games so that the odds are you will not win. But the smart gambler knows how to maximize the odds so that he will win.

The Key Principles of Winning

Following are the key principles of winning summed up:

• Know the rules of the game you are playing and all of the options available to you.

• Place bets that offer the best odds available for that game.

• Do not make an unusually large bet based on the outcome of the previous several random events. If you are playing Roulette and the last ten numbers have been EVEN, do not place a larger than usual bet on ODD; the ball just doesn't have the brains to figure out that it is time for an ODD number to appear.

If you are shooting Craps and have rolled twenty times without *sevening out*, do not place a bet on ANY SEVEN; it is still a bad bet.

• Remember that those little plastic chips and metal tokens represent real money and that the ownership of that money changes every time a bet is settled.

If you win a hand, you are not playing with the casino's money; it is your money to do with as you please. If you lose some chips, that becomes the casino's money, not some money that is still yours but is just out of reach temporarily.

• Remember the principles of good money management. If you do get a run where things go your way and you manage to double your stake, take a break, get something to drink, and look at the scenery. The game will still be there in a few minutes, and the less you play, the less opportunity you are giving the casino the chance to win back that money.

• Only gamble with money that you can afford to lose. If you get too far down, you will start making poor decisions and placing bad bets in an effort to catch up. If you lose all of your budget, pull yourself away, remind yourself that it is not your money any longer, and return on another day.

• Gamble at games you like. One of the best reasons to gamble is for the enjoyment of the game. As we have seen, the riverboats offer a variety of games with a range of betting limits. Find a game you like and a betting range that you are comfortable with. All of the odds presented in this book are based on averages over the long term.

On every cruise, there are gamblers who end up winners at each of the games available on board. With proper play, it can be you!

Appendix A: Useful Phone Numbers

ILLINOIS RIVERBOATS
Alton Belle	1-800-336-7568
Par-a-dice	1-800-332-5634
	or TicketMaster
Casino Rock Island	1-800-477-7747
Silver Eagle	1-800-723-2453
Empress	1-708-345-6789

IOWA RIVERBOATS
Casino Belle	1-800-426-5591
Mississippi Belle II	1-800-457-9975
President	1-800-262-8711

MISSISSIPPI RIVERBOATS
Isle of Capri	1-800-843-4753

STATE DEPARTMENTS OF TOURISM
Arkansas	1-800-628-8725
Illinois	1-800-223-0121
Iowa	1-800-345-4692
Louisiana	1-800-334-8626
Mississippi	1-800-647-2290
Missouri	1-800-877-1234
Gamblers Anonymous	1-800-238-7633

GAMBLING BOOK CATALOGUE
Cardoza Publishing	1-718-743-5229

Appendix B: Glossary of Gaming Terms

This list includes the basic jargon used in the gambling industry. There would be another whole book if we included all of the slang that gamblers use.

If a term is specific to a game, that is shown in parentheses at the start of the definition.

BANKER (baccarat) - one of the two hands available for each Player to bet upon. The other is PLAYER.

BLOCK BET (roulette) - a bet on a group of six numbers. The payoff is 5 to 1.

BOXCARS (craps) - double 6's on the thrown dice, a total of 12

BURN (blackjack, baccarat) - One or more cards that are dealt from the top of the deck and discarded immediately rather than being put in play. The practice of burning a card developed as one way to limit the possibilities for cheating.

BUST, BUSTED - (blackjack) - To draw to a total that is higher than 21. If a Player BUSTS, he or she loses immediately, if the Dealer BUSTS, all of the Players that did not BUST earlier in the hand win automatically.

CHECKS - Chips, the kind used at gaming tables, not the kind you eat.

COLUMN BET (roulette) - A wager placed at the bottom of one of the three columns of numbers in the Roulette layout. If the ball lands on one of the twelve numbers in that column, the payoff is 2 to 1.

COME (craps) - A bet that works exactly the same as a PASS bet but is placed after the Shooter has established a Point.

CRAPS (craps) - A total on the dice of 2, 3, or 12.

DON'T COME (craps) - A bet against the Shooter that is placed *after* a Point has been established.

DON'T PASS (craps) - A bet against the Shooter that is placed *before* a Point has been established.

DOUBLE DOWN (blackjack) - An option where the Player may double the size of the current bet and draw just one more card to the first two cards of the hand.

DOZENS BET (roulette) - A bet on the numbers 1-12, 13-24, or 25-36. The payoff is 2 to 1.

FILL (poker) - To draw the cards needed to complete one of the five-card hands (STRAIGHT, FLUSH or FULL HOUSE). For instance, if the Player has 4, 5, 6, 8 and draws a 7, it is a FILL.

FLOORMAN - One of several casino employees in charge of a group of gaming tables in the casino.

FLUSH (poker) - Five cards in the same suit, not in numerical sequence.

FOUR FLUSH (poker) - A hand with four cards of the same suit and a fifth card of any other suit.

FOUR STRAIGHT (poker) - Four cards in sequence such that one card can be added to make a straight such as 3, 4, 5 and 6.

FULL HOUSE (poker) - A hand containing three cards of the same value along with a pair of cards of a different value.

HARD (blackjack) - A hand in which there are no Ace's or the Ace's are counted as one. 10, 4, 3, A is a HARD 18 (as opposed to SOFT).

HARDWAY (craps) - When the dice total 4, 6, 8, or 10 and they each have the same number (2 and 2).

HIGH (roulette) - The numbers from 19 to 36.

HIT (blackjack) - To take a card.

INSURANCE (blackjack) - An optional bet available to Players any time the Dealer has an Ace showing. Players may bet up to one-half of the original wager that the Dealer's down card is a 10-card.

LOW (roulette) - The numbers from 1 to 18.

MARKER - A IOU check for a Player with an established line of credit with the casino.

NATURAL (baccarat, blackjack, craps) - A hand with a value of 8 or 9 in Baccarat; A Blackjack, an Ace and a 10-card in the first 2 cards in Blackjack; and in Craps, a 7 or 11 on the come-out roll.

PASS (craps) - An even money bet that wins immediately if the

Shooter's first roll is 7 or 11, loses immediately if the roll is 2, 3, or 12, and otherwise wins if the Point is rolled again before a 7.

PIT - A ring of tables in a section of the casino.

PIT BOSS - One of several casino employees who supervises a group of tables (a Pit), monitoring Dealers, processing Markers, and dealing with whatever situations arise.

PLAYER (baccarat) - One of the two hands available for the Player to bet on (the other is Banker).

POINT (craps) - The total of the dice on the Shooter's first roll if that total is not Craps (2, 3, or 12) or 7 or 11. The point will be one of 4, 5, 6, 8, 9 or 10.

PROGRESSIVE (slot machines) - One of a series of machines whose Jackpot grows as coins are played into the machine.

PUSH (blackjack, baccarat) - A tie; when the Player's hand and Dealer's hand (Banker's hand in baccarat) have the same value.

RACK - The devise tht holds chips that belong to the House and are available for paying off winning bets at a table.

RIGHT BETTOR (craps) - A Player betting with the Shooter by placing Pass and/or Come bets.

ROYAL FLUSH (poker) - A Straight Flush that runs from 10 to Ace of any one suit.

SHOE (blackjack, baccarat) - The box that holds the shuffled stack of cards.

SHOOTER (craps) - The Player who throws the dice for a turn.

SNAKE EYES (craps) - Double 1's on the dice, a total of 2.

SOFT (blackjack) - A hand in which the total includes an Ace counted as 11. A 6 is a SOFT 17 (as opposed to HARD).

SPLIT BET (roulette) - A bet placed on the line separating two numbers on the roulette table, covering both numbers. The payout is 17 to 1.

SPLIT PAIRS (blackjack) - An option available to the Player to separate the first two cards of a hand into two individual hands.

STAND (blackjack, baccarat) - To take no more cards.

STICKMAN (craps) - The casino employee who uses a long stick to retrieve the dice and offer them to the Shooter.

STRAIGHT (poker) - Five cards in numerical sequence regardless of suit. An Ace can either be high or low in a straight.

STRAIGHT FLUSH (poker) - A Straight in which all of the cards are in the same suit.

SURRENDER (blackjack) - If the Dealer has an Ace as the upcard (and does not have Blackjack), the Player may forfeit half of the current bet before taking any cards. This option is not available on the riverboats at this time, but can be found in some casinos in Atlantic City and Nevada.

TRIPS (poker) - A hand with three cards of the same value (3 of a kind) and two unrelated cards.

VIGORISH (or VIG) - (all games) - The house edge.

WRONG BETTOR (craps) - A Player betting against the Shooter by placing Don't Pass and/or Don't Come bets.

PLATINUM LOTTERY/LOTTO™

Prof. Jones' Top-Rated Computer Strategies - (IBM and Mac only)

The Platinum is the **king** of the Lottery/Lotto software, and though the Gold is powerful and brings **excellent results**, this **powerhouse strategy** is selling at an increasing rate as well. The Platinum includes all the goodies of the Gold Series **and more** and is for players **going for the max!!!** Why?

SUPER STRATEGY

This **super strategy** features over 20 of the Dimitrov Systems, the Hard Positional Analysis, all the Cluster, Bell, % of Occurrence, % of Frequency, Past Winning Numbers, Two Digit Numbers and **lots more!**

BIG FEATURES

The Platinum Lottery/Lotto™ also features an expanded cluster analysis, skip/hit chart, hot number analysis, regression analysis and **unlimited** wheeling systems!

TOP OF THE LINE

Very powerful, excellent **top-of-the-line** strategy! Includes hardbound manual, 90 day after-purchase support & replacement warranty with optional 1 year extension, and is backed by **seven years of customer satisfaction!**

HOT NUMBER ANALYSIS:
Using the skip hit chart, numbers are sorted based on their overdue status.

SKIP HIT CHART:
A true "TIME ORIENTED" sequence to allow you to actually see when each ball was picked.

EXPANDED CLUSTER ANALYSIS:
The Cluster Analysis looks at first and second clusters, 3 through 20 ball picks.

HOT NUMBER ANALYSIS
Top 30 Hottest Numbers
Analysis against 30 games

01:	42	11:	17	21:	10
02:	30	12:	34	22:	11
03:	07	13:	38	23:	12
04:	46	14:	45	24:	02
05:	33	15:	47	25:	28
06:	40	16:	49	26:	25
07:	43				
08:	23				
09:	18				
10:	27				

SKIP HIT CHART

ENTRY NUMBER	10	20	30
1	I ....*.................................*		
2	I .....*..***.............*.....*.....		
3	I .*....*............*.**.....*.*....		
4	I .....*.**.....*.....***.....**.....		
5	I **............. ...........*.*.*		

BELL CURVE ANALYSIS

CLUSTER ANALYSIS
Analysis against 20 games

NUM	Followed by 1st	2nd	NUM	Followed by 1st	2nd	NUM	Followed by 1st	2nd
01	06	--	17	20	36	34	37	--
02	06	11	18	04	25	35	39	44
03	09	04	19	20	26	36	41	43
04	16	12	20	22	21	37	46	--
05	11	38	21	22	32	38	--	--
06	08	28	22	23	26	39	06	14
07	--	--	23	27	--	40	48	--
08	13	--	24	36	--	41	09	44
09	11	28	25	31	--	42	--	--
						31	--	--
						32	46	

% of Occurence COLUMN CHARTS

To order, send $149.95 by check or money order to:
Cardoza Publishing, P.O. Box 1500, Cooper Station, New York, NY 10276

Pro-Master II Lotto and Lottery Strategies
- Prof. Jones' Ultimate Winning Strategy For Non-Computer Users -

Finally, after years of research into winning lotto tickets, Prof Jones has developed the ultimate in **winning jackpot strategies** for non-computer users! This **new powerhouse** gives you the **latest** in winning lotto strategies!

EASY TO USE - MINUTES A DAY TO WINNING JACKPOTS!
These **scientific winning systems** can be used successfully by anyone! Spend only **several minutes a day** inputting past winning numbers into the master templates and this **amazing system** quickly and **scientifically** generates the numbers that have the **best chances** of making you rich.

THE MASTER LOTTO/LOTTERY STRATEGIES AND MORE!
All the goodies of the Master Lotto/Lottery strategies - the winning systems, instruction guides, clear working template and bonus templates - are included in this **powerful winning strategy**, plus such **extra** features as the 3-Ball, 4-Ball and 6-Ball Sum Total charts. You also receive...

100 WHEELING SYSTEMS
That's right, **100** advanced Dimitrov Wheeling Systems - **double** the systems of the excellent Master Lotto/Lottery package! You'll be using the **most powerful** lotto and lottery winning systems ever designed.

BONUS
Included **free** with this **super strategy** are 15 Positional Analysis templates, 10 each 3-Ball, 4-Ball and 6-Ball Sum Total Templates and 15 Best Number templates!
EXTRA BONUS
Order now and you'll receive, **absolutely free** with your order, the extra bonus, 7 Insider Winning Tips - a conside guide to **extra winning strategies!**

$50.00 Off! This $99.95 strategy is now only $49.95 with this coupon!

To order, send ~~$99.95~~ $49.95 plus postage and handling by check or money order to:
Cardoza Publishing, P.O. Box 1500, Cooper Station, New York, NY 10276

Baccarat Master Card Counter
New Winning Strategy!

For the **first time**, Gambling Research Institute releases the **latest winning techniques** at baccarat. This **exciting** strategy, played by big money players in Monte Carlo and other exclusive locations, is based on principles that have made insiders and pros **hundreds of thousands of dollars** counting cards at blackjack - card counting!

This brand **new** strategy now applies card counting to baccarat to give you a **new winning approach,** and is designed so that any player, with just a little effort, can successfully take on the casinos at their own game - and win!

SIMPLE TO USE, EASY TO MASTER
You learn how to count cards for baccarat without the mental effort needed for blackjack! The beauty of this system is that there's no need to memorize numbers - we keep the count on the scorepad directly in front of us. Easy-to-use, play the strategy while enjoying the game!

LEARN WHEN TO BET BANKER, WHEN TO BET PLAYER
No longer will you make bets on hunches and guesses - use the GRI Baccarat Master Card Counter to determine when to bet Player and when to bet Banker. You learn the basic counts (running and true), deck favorability, when to increase bets and much more in this **winning strategy**. Plus we discuss the money management techniques important to insure your success as a baccarat card counter.

LEARN TO WIN IN JUST ONE SITTING
That's right! After **just one sitting** you'll be able to successfully learn this powerhouse strategy and use it to your advantage at the baccarat table. Be the best baccarat player at the table - the one playing the odds to **win**! Baccarat can be beaten. The Master Card Counter shows you how!

To order send just $50 by check or money order to:
Cardoza Publishing, P.O. Box 1500, Cooper Station, New York, NY 10276

Win Money at Video Poker - With the Odds!
GRI's Professional Video Poker Strategy

At last, for the **first time,** and for **serious players only,** the GRI **Professional Video Poker** strategy is released so you too can play to win! **You read it right** - this strategy gives you the **mathematical advantage** over the casino and what's more, it's **easy to learn!**

PROFESSIONAL STRATEGY SHOWS YOU HOW TO WIN WITH THE ODDS
This **powerhouse strategy,** played for **big profits** by an **exclusive** circle of **professionals,** people who make their living at the machines, is now made available to you! You too can win - with the odds - and this **winning strategy** shows you how!

HOW TO PLAY FOR A PROFIT
You'll learn the **key factors** to play on a **pro level**: which machines will turn you a profit, break-even and win rates, hands per hour and average win per hour charts, time value, team play and more! You'll also learn big play strategy, alternate jackpot play, high and low jackpot play and key strategies to follow.

WINNING STRATEGIES FOR ALL MACHINES
This **comprehensive, advanced pro package** not only shows you how to win money at the 8-5 progressives, but also, the **winning strategies** for 10s or better, deuces wild, joker's wild, flat-top, progressive and special options features.

BE A WINNER IN JUST ONE DAY
In just one day, after learning our strategy, you will have the skills to **consistently win money** at video poker - with the odds. The strategies are easy to use under practical casino conditions.

FREE BONUS - PROFESSIONAL PROFIT EXPECTANCY FORMULA ($15 VALUE)
For serious players, we're including this free bonus essay which explains the professional profit expectancy principles of video poker and how to relate them to real dollars and cents in your game.
  To order send just $50 by check or money order to:
    Cardoza Publishing, P.O. Box 1500, Cooper Station, New York, NY 10276

The Cardoza Craps Master
Exclusive Offer!
(Not Available Anywhere Else)
Three Big Strategies!

Here It is! **At last**, the **secrets** of the **Grande-Gold Power Sweep, Molliere's Monte Carlo Turnaround** and the **Montarde-D'Girard Double Reverse** - three big strategies - are made available and presented for the **first time anywhere!** These powerful strategies are designed for the serious craps player, one wishing to bring the best odds and strategies to hot tables, cold tables and choppy tables.

1. The Grande-Gold Power Sweep (Hot Table Strategy)

This **dynamic strategy** takes maximum advantage of hot tables and shows the player methods of amassing small **fortunes quickly** when numbers are being thrown fast and furious. The Grande-Gold stresses aggressive betting on wagers the house has no edge on! This previously unreleased strategy will make you a powerhouse at a hot table.

2. Molliere's Monte Carlo Turnaround (Cold Table Strategy)

For the player who likes betting against the dice, Molliere's Monte Carlo Turnaround shows how to turn a cold table into hot cash. Favored by an exclusive circle of professionals who will play nothing else, the uniqueness of this strongman strategy is that the vast majority of bets **give absolutely nothing away to the casino!**

3. The Montarde-D'Girard Double Reverse (Choppy Table Strategy)

This **new** strategy is the **latest development** and the **most exciting strategy** to be designed in recent years. **Learn how** to play the optimum strategies against the tables when the dice run hot and cold (a choppy table) with no apparent reason. **The Montarde-d'Girard Double Reverse** shows you how you can **generate big profits** while less knowledgeable players are ground out by choppy dice. And, of course, the majority of our bets give nothing away to the casino!

BONUS!!!

Order now, and you'll receive **The Craps Master-Professional Money Management Formula** ($15 value) **absolutely free!** Necessary for serious players and **used by the pros**, the **Craps Master Formula** features the unique **stop-loss ladder**.

The Above Offer is Not Available Anywhere Else. You Must Order Here.

To order send ~~$75~~ $50 by check or money order to:

Cardoza Publishing, P.O. Box 1500, Cooper Station, New York, NY 10276

Win Money at Blackjack! Special Introductory Offer!
THE CARDOZA BASE COUNT STRATEGY

Finally, a count strategy has been developed which allows the average player to play blackjack like a **pro**! Actually, this strategy isn't new. The Cardoza Base Count Strategy has been used successfully by graduates of the Cardoza School of Blackjack for years. But **now**, for the **first time**, this "million dollar" strategy, which was only available previously to those students attending the school, is available to **you**!

FREE VACATIONS! A SECOND INCOME?

You bet! Once you learn this strategy, you will have the skills to **consistently win big money** at blackjack. The longer you play, the more you make. The casino's bankroll is yours for the taking.

BECOME AN EXPERT IN TWO DAYS

Why struggle over complicated strategies that aren't as powerful? In just **two days or less**, you can learn the Cardoza Base Count and be among the best blackjack players. Friends will look up to you in awe - for you will be a **big winner** at blackjack.

BEAT ANY SINGLE OR MULTIPLE DECK GAME

We show you how, with just a **little effort**, you can effectively beat any single or multiple deck game. You'll learn how to count cards, how to use advanced betting and playing strategies, how to make money on insurance bets, and much, much, more in this 6,000 word, chart-filled strategy package.

SIMPLE TO USE, EASY TO MASTER

You too can win! The **power** of the Cardoza Base Count strategy is not only in its **computer-proven** winning results but also in its **simplicity**. Many beginners who thought card counting was too difficult have given the Cardoza Base Count the acid test - they have **won consistently** in casinos around the world.

The Cardoza Base Count strategy is designed so that **any player** can win under practical casino conditions. **No need** for a mathematical mind or photographic memory. **No need** to be bogged down by calculations. Keep **only one number** in your head at any time. The casinos will never suspect that you're a counter.

BONUS!

But to provide extra precautions, the fact-filled 1,500 word essay, "How Not to Get Barred," is included **free**. Here, you'll learn the all-important techniques of projecting a losing image, role playing, and other skills to maximize your profit potential.

EXTRA BONUS!!

Rush your order in now, for we're also including, **absolutely free**, the 1,000 word essay "How to Disguise the Fact that You're an Expert." Among other **inside information** contained here, you'll learn about the psychology of the pit bosses and receive a comprehensive guide on how they spot counters.

As an **introductory offer to readers of this book**, the Cardoza Base Count Strategy, which has netted graduates of the Cardoza School of Blackjack **substantial sums** of **money**, is being offered for **only $50**! To order, send $50 by check or money order to:
Cardoza Publishing, P.O. Box 1500, Cooper Station, New York, NY 10276

WIN MONEY PLAYING BLACKJACK! - MAIL THIS COUPON TODAY!

Yes, I want to **win big money** at blackjack. Please **rush** me the Cardoza Base Count Strategy. Enclosed is a check or money order for $50. I understand that the bonus and extra bonus essays are included **absolutely free**.

Enclosed is a check or money order for $50 (plus postage and handling) made out to:

Cardoza Publishing
P.O. Box 1500, Cooper Station, New York, NY 10276

Please include $3.50 postage and handling for U.S. & Canada, other countries $7.00. Orders outside United States, money order payable in U.S. dollars on U.S. bank only.

NAME _____

ADDRESS _____

CITY _____ STATE _____ ZIP _____

Offer valid only through this coupon = 30 Day Money Back Guarantee! RIV

127

CARDOZA SCHOOL OF BLACKJACK
- Home Instruction Course - $200 OFF! -

At last, after years of secrecy, the **previously unreleased** lesson plans, strategies and playing tactics formerly available only to members of the Cardoza School of Blackjack are now available to the general public - and at substantial savings. **Now**, you can **learn at home,** and at your own convenience. Like the full course given at the school, the home instruction course goes **step-by-step** over the winning concepts. We'll take you from layman to **pro.**

MASTER BLACKJACK - Learn what it takes to be a **master player.** Be a **powerhouse,** play with confidence, impunity, and **with the odds** on your side. Learn to be a **big winner** at blackjack.

MAXIMIZE WINNING SESSIONS - You'll **learn how** to take a good winning session and make a **blockbuster** out of it, but just as important, you'll learn to cut your losses. Learn exactly when to end a session. We cover everything from the psychological and emotional aspects of play (through the **eye of profitability**) to protection of big wins. The advice here could be worth **hundreds (or thousands) of dollars** in one session alone. Take our guidelines seriously.

ADVANCED STRATEGIES - You'll learn the **latest** in advanced winning strategies. Learn about the **ten-factor**, the **Ace-factor**, the effects of rules variations, how to protect against dealer blackjacks, the winning strategies for single and multiple deck games and how each affects you; the **true count**, the multiple deck true count variations, and much, much more.

And, of course, you'll receive the full Cardoza Base Count Strategy package.

$200 OFF - LIMITED OFFER - The Cardoza School of Blackjack home instruction course, which is retailed at $295 (or $895 if taken through the school) is available now for just $95.

BONUS! - **Rush** your order in **now**, for we're also including, **absolutely free**, the 1,000 word essays, "How to Disguise the Fact that You're an Expert", and "How Not to Get Barred". Among other **inside information** contained here, you'll learn about the psychology of the pit bosses and receive a comprehensive guide on how they spot counters.

To order, send $95 by check or money order to:

Cardoza Publishing, P.O. Box 1500, Cooper Station, New York, NY 10276